Home Bakebook of *Natural* Breads &Goodies

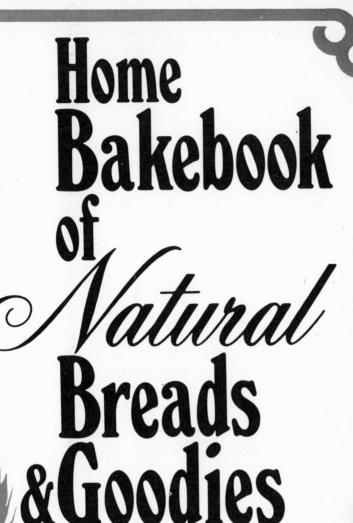

Home Bakebook of *Natural* Breads &Goodies

by Sandra & Bruce Sandler

illustrations by
Kathie Longinotti

STACKPOLE BOOKS

HOME BAKEBOOK OF NATURAL BREADS AND GOODIES

Published by
STACKPOLE BOOKS
Cameron and Kelker Streets
Harrisburg, Pennsylvania 17105

*In the interests of conservation, this
book is printed on 100% recycled paper.*

Printed in the U.S.A.

Library of Congress Cataloging in Publication Data

Sandler, Sandra, 1945-
    Home bakebook of natural breads and goodies.

    1. Baking. I. Sandler, Bruce, 1943-   joint
author. II. Title.
TX765.S26   641.7'1   70-179602
ISBN 0-8117-0801-2

CONTENTS

INTRODUCTION

WE'VE ALL HEARD people praise the delicious breads and rolls grandma used to bake. Most people, however, believe that home breadbaking went out with grandma's wood burning stove. True, it is almost frightening to imagine baking today in a wood burning stove, but modern ovens have eliminated much of the work of baking day, and the products are just as good—or better!

We're not anybody's grandma and grandpa—not for a while at least—but we do enjoy our own home baked breads and goodies. Fresh baked whole grain breads are a most satisfying food. They fill the kitchen with a marvelous aroma and fill the house with love. Few things are as enjoyable as spreading fresh sweet butter on hot bread straight from the oven. And, few store or bakery bought breads are quite as nutritious as home baked breads with whole grains and organic ingredients.

Bread is the staff of life, or at least it's supposed to be. The pale, squishy supermarket product certainly cannot be the food that supports life. It has all it can do to support a knife of firm peanut butter. However, breads baked at home with whole grains do deserve to be called the staff of life. They provide all the nutritional value of the foods from which they are made. The bread found on supermarket shelves is called enriched. And it is. During processing, approximately 21 vital nutrients are removed from the flour. Enriching the bread consists of putting four (4) nutrients back into the processed flour. There is obviously something missing.

We have implied that home baking is not as difficult as it once was, but making truly good baked products is still not as simple as adding 1 cup of water to the mix, stirring, and baking for 30 minutes. We have written *Home Bakebook of Natural Breads and Goodies* to provide the beginning baker with the information necessary to smooth the road to baking success. The experienced baker will find information useful to easing the transition to whole grain baking.

The nutritional value of the food we eat is—or should be—an important consideration. This topic will be discussed. In addition, some easy ways of supplementing the nutritional value of baked goods are suggested.

No book is ever the final word on a subject. This one is no exception. We have made no attempt to provide you with all the bread, cake, cookie, etc. recipes, since it is surely an impossible task. There is a tremendous amount of room for creativity in home baking. We have given you the fundamentals. From here, you can devise new recipes and alter old ones to suit both your taste and fancy.

RICK AND SANDY SANDLER

CHAPTER 1

WHOLE GRAINS
AND ORGANIC FOODS

ALL OF THE recipes in this book are based upon the use of whole grain flours—whole wheat, whole rye, soy flour, cornmeal, etc. Ordinary bleached white flour can be substituted for whole grain flours, but there will be three major differences. First, the recipe may require slightly different proportions of ingredients. Second, the texture of the bread will change. Third, the bread will not be as nutritious and will not taste as good.

WHY WHOLE GRAINS?

Whole grains, as the name implies, are milled in such a way that the entire kernel of grain is ground and finds its way into the resulting flour. Ordinary white flour, on the other hand, contains only a portion of the kernel, the endosperm. This is basically carbohydrates. Most notably, and importantly, the wheat germ is missing and it is the germ that makes bread a wholesome and nutritious food.

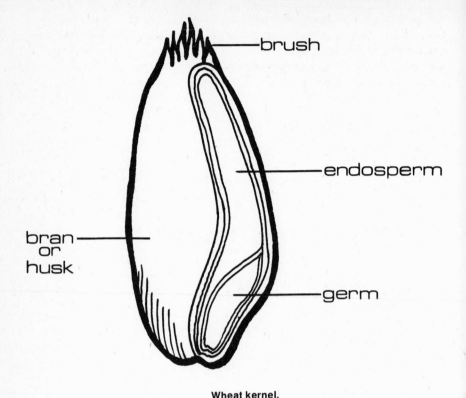

Wheat kernel.

The whole wheat kernel is made up of three edible parts. The bran is the covering of the grain and is rich in carbohydrates, B vitamins, proteins, and minerals—particularly iron. In the center of the kernel lies the carbohydrate-rich endosperm, the pride of refined white flour. The germ is really the embryo of a new wheat plant, and it is logical that the nutritional riches be concentrated here. The germ contains valuable quantities of B vitamins (particularly thiamine), protein, fat, vitamin E, minerals, and carbohydrates.

Until fairly recently, all flour was stone-ground. That is, the grain was crushed by the rotation of a millstone which was usually driven by water power. Most of us are familiar with the picturesque old mill situated on a pond. The gigantic water wheel supplied power for the massive stone within. With the advent of new milling methods in the early 1900's, all of this began to change.

The change may have been stimulated by the increasing population, or by changes in its living habits. It was made possible by the availability of new sources of power and advancing technology. It was no longer necessary to locate mills by sources of running water. The result was the development of a milling method which no longer made use of the millstone. Grain was now made into flour by the use of steel rollers. These were designed so the germ and bran could be easily removed. This development made it more economical to remove the germ and bran from the flour.

The evolution from whole grain to white flour came about because of the economic advantages to the processor which result from

Old water mill.

removing the bran and the germ. Because the germ contains fat, whole wheat flour tends to spoil when stored for long periods. If the germ is removed, however, the flour may be stored for considerably longer. As the factories which produced flour became centralized, the time between the grinding of the flour and its purchase by the customer—who might be located thousands of miles away—increased. Since the manufacturer could realize considerable economies by centralizing his production facilities, there was considerable incentive for him to find a method of overcoming the storage problem. This problem was overcome at the nutritional expense of the customer.

Removing the germ from the wheat not only permitted the manufacturer to store the flour for longer periods, but it also gave him another product to sell. With the germ contained in the flour, the manufacturer has only flour to sell, but if the germ is separated, it may be sold separately. When the bran is also separated in the milling process—and it is— there are three products to sell. So instead of selling only one product, the manufacturer sells three products and realizes three profits. In addition, by stripping the flour of its nutritional qualities, a ready market for the germ and bran is created.

Flour from which the germ and bran have been removed (white or unbleached flour) is, for all intents and purposes, nutritionally worthless. It is nearly void of the vitamins and minerals which are found in the whole wheat kernel. For this reason alone, white and unbleached flours should be avoided. They provide bulk, but little nutritional value.

Not only are non-whole grains lacking in nutritional value, they may be detrimental to health. White flour is said to be a major cause of constipation in the United States. Unfortunate as this may be for those prone to such affliction, it is not without blessing to the manufacturers selling wheat bran since the latter is an extremely effective cure. Hence, the flour manufacturer is in an enviable position: within his line of products, one cures certain difficulties caused by another.

In addition, wheat germ is sold for its nutritional and healthful qualities. This is a rather tacit admission that the flour from which the germ has been removed is lacking in the very qualities that the germ is meant to supplement. It seems senseless and wasteful to purchase three separate products to get the nutritional benefits available in a single product. And it is much more expensive.

Besides the nutritional aspect, whole grain breads are almost a completely different food from "enriched" white bread. Like good European peasant bread, they are firm and not susceptible to squishing when touched. Nor does a hole appear when semi-soft butter or peanut butter is spread. It is a coarser, full-bodied, and full-flavored loaf that smells and tastes like "enriched" white bread never can. One can now have rye bread that is really rye bread, rather than being slightly rye-flavored wheat bread. Incredible? Check the label on packaged "rye bread" at the store. Under federal law, the ingredients are listed in order of the amount present in the product. The ingredients list in "rye bread" invariably begins "enriched white flour, etc." The same is generally true of whole wheat bread.

WHY ORGANIC INGREDIENTS?

Organic ingredients are those that are raised, harvested, and stored *without* the use of chemical fertilizers, pesticides, preservatives, or fumigants.

During the last twenty years agriculture has come to depend on chemical fertilizers to replace what they take from the soil and destroy, and on pesticides which indiscriminately kill insects, small animals, birds, and an occasional human. Sugar water is fed to bees to increase honey production, despite the fact that quality and food value suffer. Livestock are given growth hormones and antibiotics to ensure their faster delivery to market. Chickens are administered hormones to stimulate growth and increase egg production. Consumer demand for year-round availability of all foods in all forms has brought about an availability of almost all foods—with preservatives.

Read the labels and small print: "BHA and BHT added to preserve freshness," "sulphur dioxide added," "contains sodium nitrate," "butylated hydroxyanisole," etc. Scratch the skin of a "fresh" turnip or rutabaga during the winter or early spring. Yes, it's coated with paraffin. Flour and sugar are refined and stripped of all their nutritional value in order to achieve the snowy-white look of purity—pure gunk! Organic ingredients are what these are *not*.

Although no one is really sure how chemical fertilizers, pesticides, preservatives, and hormones affect us on a long term basis, there is scientific evidence indicating what can happen with short term high dosages. The ban on cyclamates not long ago following the discovery that they produced cancer in laboratory animals is an obvious example. Evidence is also beginning to accumulate which indicates that the nitrate additives routinely used as preservatives of meat products may also be carcinogenic. Many of the additives and preservatives routinely used in our food are assumed to be safe—but no one knows for sure. Cyclamates were also *assumed* to be safe.

The evidence is clearer with regard to pesticides. They are poisons. It has been proven that pesticides have caused at least one species—the Peregrine Falcon—to be on the verge of extinction and have been responsible for marked increases in mortality rates in other species. Scientific research has found that all living things have pesticide residues in their bodies. Furthermore, evidence is beginning to indicate that pesticides may have subtle and unsuspected effects on the behavior and physiology of animals and man. The evidence is merely suggestive, but what it suggests is not comforting. And neither is the report that the amount of DDT in human milk is higher than the amount permitted in cows' milk by the United States Government.

It is possible that there is nothing harmful about all the chemicals which find their way into us through our food and medicines. Research may ultimately prove them safe within certain limits. Then again, maybe it won't. We prefer to take a conservative approach. We *know* organic foods are safe.

Organic foods—whether wheat or beef—are raised without the use of chemical fertilizers, pesticides, antibiotics, etc. Organic farming is as much a philosophy of life as a method of farming. The organic farmer works with nature, not against her. He accepts the concept that he is part of a closed system and must behave accordingly. If he takes nutrients and minerals out of the earth in the course of raising his crops, he must replace them. But he replaces them with natural substances which would otherwise be wasted. Thus, manure, vegetable matter, sawdust, and other organic material are returned to the earth. By recycling this material the organic farmer completes the cycle and maintains balance in the closed system in which he lives and works.

The general principles of organic farming apply to each ingredient we use in baking. A major difficulty for the consumer is to be sure that the ingredients he is buying are strictly organically raised, stored, and packaged.

Yeast most often comes packaged with "BHA to preserve freshness." In the experience of many purchasers, yeast without BHA cannot be bought in grocery stores, but must be obtained at one of the many health food stores or mail-order houses. Better yet, keep a pot of sourdough starter. Flour has been discussed to some extent. Only whole grain flours with no preservatives should be used. White flour, even enriched white flour, contains only a small fraction of the food value of whole grain flours. If sugar is used as the sweetener, it should be raw sugar, not white granulated sugar, not powdered sugar, not even brown or dark brown sugar.

Molasses or honey may be substituted for sugar, but beware of the

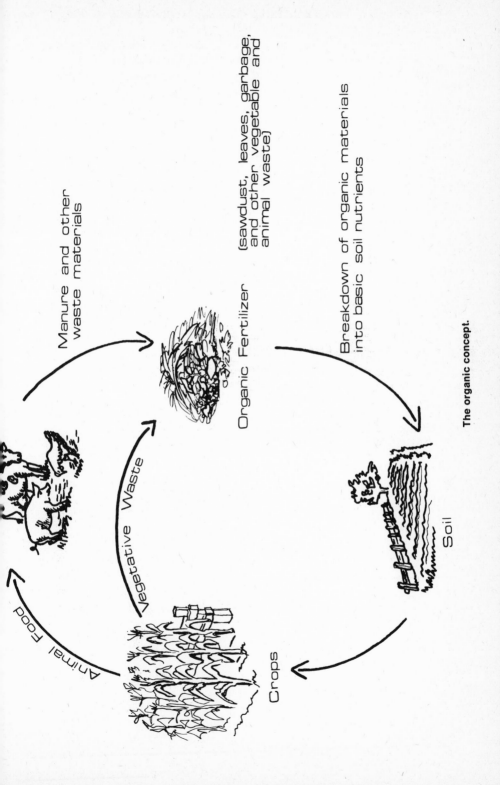

Manure and other waste materials

Organic Fertilizer (sawdust, leaves, garbage, and other vegetable and animal waste)

Breakdown of organic materials into basic soil nutrients

Vegetative Waste

Animal Food

Crops

Soil

The organic concept.

sulphur generally found in light molasses or the honey from bees fed sugar water. Liquid shortening should be cold-pressed oils. Supermarket vegetable oils are obtained through chemical processes in which chemicals are added to the raw ingredients to help draw the oils out. It is very difficult to ascertain whether most of the other ingredients used—soy flour or beans, potatoes, rice, herbs, nuts, fruit, and other produce—have been organically grown and marketed. Here, one must depend on the word of a reputable farmer, merchant, or mail-order house.

The surface of the organic method has been merely touched. The interested reader will have no difficulty locating a wealth of material on organic farming and organic living. The point is that organic ingredients are different, and probably better. They are also a little costlier and more difficult to obtain. If one is lucky, sources of supply can be located nearby—perhaps a health food store, an old water mill, or organic farmers. If none of these sources exist, there are a number of mail-order organic food establishments. Generally their service is quick and their prices are fairly reasonable. A list of sources has been included at the end of the book. Of course, the only assurance one has that the product is strictly organically-grown is the word of the business firm dealt with. But firms in the organic mail-order business are generally reputable and committed to the organic concept. Still, the importance of dealing with a reputable firm should not be minimized.

There is another way of meeting some of one's needs for organic ingredients. He may grow his own. In most cases, one will only be able to grow a few of the things needed or wanted. But why not grow those few? Even those living in a city apartment can grow a few things on window sills. A few pots of herbs will provide some of the ingredients for herb bread, and they will come in handy in dozens of dishes. Try it!

While it is true that whole grains and organic ingredients generally cost more than processed ones, substantial savings to the home baker may be realized by careful price shopping. Health food stores are invariably expensive. Certain products may be cheaper there, however, after postage and handling charges are added to the cost of goods ordered by mail. Buying from local organic farmers and millers is most often the source of greatest savings.

A comparison of the cost of one loaf of "Basic Whole Wheat Bread" has been calculated using processed ingredients versus natural ingredients, or whole grains and organic products. Here are some cost estimates based on the average price of comparable brands.

Recipe (2 loaves)	Processed Ingredients	Natural Ingredients
1 T. dry yeast	$ .07	$ .02
3 1/2 c. water	-	-
2 T. sugar	.003	.01 (raw sugar)
2 t. salt	.003	.013 (sea salt)
8 c. flour	.22	.38 (whole wheat)
	$ .296	$ .423
	2 loaves	2 loaves
	= $.15 per loaf	= $ .21 per loaf

While the cost of using natural ingredients is higher, the saying, "You get what you pay for" applies in terms of nutritional value.

(*Note:* Here and throughout book: c—cup   t—teaspoon   T—tablespoon.)

CHAPTER 2

PREPARING TO BAKE

AN UNDERSTANDING OF the ingredients and techniques used in baking—why they are used and what they contribute to the finished product—adds to the enjoyment of baking. This chapter offers information contributing to that enjoyment.

INGREDIENTS

All baked goods consist of two basic ingredients: flour and a liquid. This combination alone will result in a bread product, but a very basic and bland one. Other ingredients are added to sweeten, flavor, and leaven. The result is a variety of baked goods ranging from breads to cakes, and including such diverse things as pancakes, rolls, and cookies.

Flour

Flour is perhaps the most basic and most important ingredient in baking. Many different grains, beans, and nuts are ground into flour and are available for baking. The variety is almost limitless. Of these, *wheat* is unquestionably the most important because of its gluten content.

It is thought that gluten develops from the interaction of glutenin and gliadin. In the presence of moisture and handling, these substances interact to form gluten. A number of grains have the ability to develop gluten, but only wheat is able to develop a gluten with the elastic qualities necessary to permit the dough to expand and still trap and hold the gas given off by the yeast. Hence wheat has the unique ability to develop gluten in its most complete form.

Different types of wheat vary in the amount of gluten they contain. For bread baking, a wheat with a high gluten content is desired. Hard wheat has a higher gluten content than soft wheat. The former is sometimes referred to as bread flour and it should be used with yeast breads, including sourdoughs, rather than with quick breads and pie pastry. But bread flour is difficult to obtain so it may have to be purchased through one of the mail-order houses listed in the appendix. Soft wheat is often referred to as cake flour. The lower gluten content of this wheat results in a product with a fluffier texture, making it unsuitable for yeast breads. All-purpose flour is a blend of both hard and soft wheats. As the name implies, it can be used for all types of baking.

Rye, barley, rice, and other flours contain some gluten. However, they do not contain any gliadin and it is this substance which gives gluten its elasticity. Without gliadin, the gluten is not the same type as that found in wheat. It does not develop the elasticity necessary to trap the yeast gas and support the leavening process. If these flours are used without wheat or if they are used with very little wheat, the texture of the end product will be quite different from wheat bread. As a way around this problem and to maintain the wheat bread texture, commercial bakers use only about 15% rye flour in their rye breads.

While good 100% whole rye bread *can* be baked without wheat flour, all other flours—rice, barley, millet, potato, buckwheat, etc.—require wheat flour to produce satisfactory yeast bread. Rice, barley, millet, and potato flours may be used interchangeably in any recipe. These flours can replace about a fourth of the wheat flour in yeast bread recipes. Rye bread baked with no wheat flour is a heavy and delightfully nutty product. Where the development of gluten is unimportant in the leavening process, as in cakes, cookies, and other desserts, rye flour can almost always be substituted successfully. Cookies are particularly amenable to substitutions by other flours. Because of the versatility of wheat flour, it may *always* be used when other flours are not available.

Oats

Oats are usually available rolled or steel cut. Quick cooking or instant oats found in the supermarkets generally have the germ removed and are thus not desirable. Old fashioned rolled oats with the germ intact is recommended. Steel cut oats look like coarse grits and require a much longer cooking time than do rolled oats. They are often the preferred form because unlike rolled oats, they are not heated in processing. Steel cut oats are most often used as a hot cereal, although they may be used in breads and cookies and as a stretcher or supplement in meat and vegetable dishes. To substitute for rolled oats in breads and cookies, replace one measure of rolled oats with one-half measure of steel cut oats and one-half measure of whole wheat or rye flour.

Peanut Flour

Often rather difficult to obtain, peanut flour is easily made in the home with raw or unsalted roasted peanuts. Place about one cup of shelled peanuts at a time in a blender until the texture resembles that of coarse cornmeal. Do not grind any longer or it may begin to turn into peanut butter. Other nut flours may be made in the same way.

Cornmeal

Cornmeal is packaged as plain or self-rising. Actually, baking powder or soda is added to "self-rising" cornmeal; it is not a special strain of corn that rises by itself! Only plain cornmeal is specified in the recipes in this book and white and yellow cornmeal may be used interchangeably. Yellow cornmeal is generally preferred, however, because of its slightly higher vitamin value.

Flour—Amounts to Use and Storage

Invariably, the bread recipes in most books call for an approximate amount of flour; for example, 6-7 cups. There are two basic reasons for this. First, the moisture content of the flour varies according to the way it is stored and with the humidity. Since the exact amount of flour required is a function of its moisture content, it is not possible to state exactly how much flour is needed. Second, whole grain flours are usually not sifted in order to prevent the separation of the bran and germ from the endosperm. Rather, whole grain flours are gently tossed in a bowl or canister, then measured out. The amount of flour in one cup may vary slightly with its compactness or density. The section on baking techniques later in this chapter will help one determine, however, when enough flour has been added.

It has already been mentioned that whole grain flours will not keep as long as the non-nutritious white flours. This is not likely to cause any difficulty to the home baker. Flour storage qualities are important mainly to manufacturers and wholesalers having considerable investments in stock. But freshly-ground whole grain flours will keep for periods sufficiently long so that the home baker need not be particularly concerned about spoilage. If there are any doubts, flours may be stored in the refrigerator or freezer. This also offers adequate protection against any insects.

Leavening

Yeast is the ingredient which causes bread to rise, be it yeast bread or sourdough. It is generally agreed that the discovery of leavened bread came about quite accidentally when a mixture of flour and water was left standing and became invaded by wild yeasts. The result was the first sourdough. The bread which was baked from it was such an improvement over the flat, hard, and tough breads baked previously that the idea caught on. Today, special strains of yeast are available for use in yeast breads and sourdoughs. These yeasts are more active than wild yeast but do not impart to the bread any undesirable flavor as do their wild cousins.

Yeasts are tiny living organisms. They feed on sugars, in the process producing alcohol and carbon dioxide. The carbon dioxide released in this process is trapped by the glutens, causing the dough to rise. Yeasts are extremely sensitive to temperature. They are most active when the temperature is between $78°$—$82°$ F. Their activity ceases, essentially, if they are stored below $50°$ F., but storage at cold temperatures will not harm them. When returned to a warm temperature, they will become active again.

Yeasts begin to die at about $120°$ F., and it is safe to assume that they have all been destroyed if exposed to temperatures over $140°$ F. Because yeasts are easily killed by high temperatures, it is necessary to be sure that liquids in which they are used are kept below the danger point. Hot water from the tap can be close to $180°$ F. When the recipe specifies *warm* water, it means water no hotter than 110° F. Experience will teach what this feels like.

It has been mentioned that yeasts feed on sugar. When yeasts are added to a flour and water mixture, they convert starch in the flour to sugar. The addition of a little sugar to the mixture *increases* the activity of the yeast; too much sugar *retards* it. Salt also inhibits yeast activity, hence, it must be used judiciously.

Yeasts may be dissolved in milk as well as water. If milk is used, however, certain rules should be observed. Whole milk should not be used since the fat in it has a tendency to coat the yeast and prevent it from dissolving. If non-pasteurized milk is used, it must be scalded *before* the yeast is dissolved in it. Scalding kills the bacteria present in milk and thereby prevents their undesirable interaction with the yeast. If pasteurized milk is used, scalding is unnecessary.

Yeast comes in two forms: moist cakes and dry. The cakes are all but impossible to obtain and consequently are not used in recipes in this book. Dry yeast may be purchased in individual packets in the supermarket. This yeast, however, is usually chemically treated to improve its storage qualities. Untreated dry yeast may be somewhat more difficult to obtain. It may be necessary to get it at a local health food store or from one of the mail order houses dealing with organic foods. If stored in the freezer or refrigerator, this yeast will keep for a considerable length of time—so long, in fact, that one will wonder why it is necessary to add anything to it at all to improve its storage qualities.

Although other yeasts are available, it is important to use only baking yeast for leavening. Brewer's yeast, sold as a non-viable vitamin supplement, has no leavening power. It is, however, very high in vitamins, especially B complex. It may be added to bread recipes to improve the nutritional content.

Baking Powders

Baking powders are used to produce a leavening, or rising action, in cakes, pancakes, and other batter breads. It is used instead of yeast when a light, crumbly texture is desired. No kneading or long proofing is needed because the rising action that results from baking powder is due to the release of gas which then becomes trapped by the gluten in the dough or batter. Whereas the gas given off by yeast is the result of a metabolic process, the gas given off by baking powder is the result of a chemical reaction. All baking powders contain an acid and an alkaline material. When water is added, these materials interact to produce a gas.

Baking powders differ in the acid ingredient that is used. They can be classified into three main types: tartrate, phosphate, and sodium aluminum sulfate. Some people object to the use of any baking powder or soda. The reason for this is that the same chemical reaction which produces the gas necessary for rising the bread or cake can also produce gastric distress in persons eating the finished product. More commonly, though, the baking powders containing aluminum compounds are considered most objectionable.

Baking powders may be either single-acting or double-acting. A single-acting baking powder releases the greatest amount of its carbon dioxide upon contact with moisture in the cold dough. A little additional gas is released during baking. Double-acting baking powders release a little gas upon contact with moisture in the cold dough; more gas is triggered by heat during baking. Double-acting baking powders often contain aluminum compounds, nevertheless it is possible to purchase them without aluminum.

Liquids

Liquids serve two purposes in baking. First, they provide the moisture necessary for the creation of the dough and the development of the gluten. Second, they serve as the medium for the activation of the rising agent used, whether it be yeast or baking powder. Water or milk is most often used as the liquid, but fruit and vegetable juices may also be used. Fresh milk or reconstituted powdered milk may be used interchangeably. Powdered milk, which is much less expensive than fresh milk, is sold both in instant and non-instant forms. Although non-instant milk powder takes a little longer to dissolve, it is much higher in protein than the instant powder. If juices are used in yeast breads, the yeast should be first dissolved in about 1/4 cup of warm water.

Salt

Salt, which enhances the flavor of foods to which it is added, serves the same function in baking. Salt should be used sparingly in yeast breads because it inhibits the growth of yeasts. Sea salt is preferred to regular table salt.

Sweetenings

Sugar immediately comes to mind as a sweetening agent, but it is by no means the only one, or the best. Honey and molasses may also be used to sweeten baked goods.

Sugar, as referred to in this book is *raw sugar*. Raw sugar is composed of large, square beige crystals. Raw sugar is not the same as brown sugar; raw sugar is unrefined. It is the residue that is left after molasses has been extracted. Brown sugar is the result of further refining and processing. The highly processed and refined white sugar so widely available has been stripped of its vitamin content during the refining process. As a result, the body must call on its vitamin reserves in order to convert its sucrose to the glucose which it can use. Raw sugar, however, still has its vitamin content intact. As a result, it is easier to digest. If necessary, white sugar may be substituted for raw sugar, measure for measure.

There are basically three types of molasses: unsulphured molasses, sulphured molasses, and blackstrap molasses. Molasses is the residue of sugar refining. The molasses used for cooking and baking comes from sugar cane, since sugar beet molasses has an unpleasant taste and smell. Light molasses is generally preserved with sulphur, an undesirable additive, and should be avoided. Fortunately, it is easy to obtain unsulphured and blackstrap molasses.

Molasses can be substituted for sugar in order to vary the flavor of the finished product. In addition to the distinctive and pleasant flavor, molasses also imparts a rich, brown color to baked goods. When substituting molasses for sugar, it is best to use no more than 3/4 cup of molasses for each cup of sugar. Using molasses also reduces the amount of other liquids which are required in a recipe by about 1/4 cup for each cup of molasses added. Honey may be used as a substitute for molasses. It can usually be substituted measure for measure, but if a very sweet honey is used, only about 3/4 as much honey may be necessary. As with molasses, reduce the amount of other liquids by about 1/4 cup when substituting honey for sugar. With raw sugar used as a molasses substitute, use 1 1/4 cups sugar for each cup of molasses and increase the amount of liquid in the recipe by 1/4 cup.

Honey is used in its pure form; it is not necessary to process or refine it before eating it or using it in baking. Its range of colors, flavors, and consistencies available are practically limitless and depend on the flowers visited by the bees. Honey is almost invariably sweeter than sugar. Because of this, less honey is required when substituting for sugar. Use only 1/2 to 3/4 the amount of sugar called for, depending on the sweetness of the honey. Experience will help to determine the relative sweetness of a particular honey. To substitute raw sugar for honey, replace 1 cup very sweet honey with about 2 cups raw sugar. For a cup of honey that is less sweet, only about 1 1/3 cups raw sugar may be necessary. Honey tends to make baked goods brown faster, so an oven temperature no higher than 325° F. should be used. Some apiaries have taken to feeding sugar water to the bees in order to increase production. Honey is also often processed with sulphur preservatives. None of this is necessary or desirable. If organically produced honey is available, it is definitely to be preferred.

Fats and Oils

Oils are added to bread in small amounts to yield a richer product. If available, cold-pressed liquid oils are preferred. "Cold-pressed" refers to the method used for extracting the oil from the original substance, whether it is derived from peanuts, corn, soybeans, or sunflower seeds. Cold-pressing extracts the oils through the use of pressure, with care being taken to prevent heat from building up. This method tends to be a bit slower and more expensive than some of the alternatives which are available, and hence is rarely used by large commercial processors. Most liquid oils found in the grocery stores are extracted by means of a chemical process, this being faster and cheaper.

Butter is the queen of fats. Its esteem has been upheld over the centuries. It is used as a shortening, either alone or in combination with another fat such as lard. Butter cannot be duplicated in flavor and richness, and it also imparts a beautiful mellow brown color to the crust of bread and pastries. Unfortunately, many people have reduced or eliminated butter from their diets in favor of margarine in the mistaken belief that by so doing, they were reducing the amount of hydrogenated fat in their diet. It is true that butter is a hydrogenated fat and that corn oil, for example, is not. That is, it is not hydrogenated when it is in liquid form. When it is made into margarine, however, it is hydrogenated. Unfortunately, the wholesome goodness of margarine exists more in the advertising copy and its implications rather than in the margarine itself.

Margarine does contain the same amount of fat as butter, and can be substituted one for one. Margarine is cheaper than butter, but certainly does not compare in taste and flavor. When used in baking, it produces a product of slightly different texture.

Those who decide to use margarine should read the label carefully. Many margarines are liberally laced with an impressive collection of stabilizers and preservatives. Ironically, some of the less expensive brands appear to be the only ones without these additives.

Lard is rendered pork fat. It is readily available in supermarkets, but it is also full of chemical preservatives. Unless one renders his own lard, he will probably have to choose between doing without or using the supermarket variety. The highly crystalline structure of lard allows it to cut into flour, and it produces flaky textures in pie crusts. This same characteristic, however, makes it less desirable in cakes.

Vegetable shortenings are also widely available and invariably contain preservatives. They are not used in any of the recipes in this book.

Flavorings

Any of a number of things may be used to add flavor to bread. Herbs and spices, nuts, fruit, and vegetables may all be used to bring out different flavors and effects, as well as adding variety to breads, cakes, cookies, and other goodies.

Many of the different nuts—pecans, walnuts, almonds, hazelnuts— may be used interchangeably in most recipes. They are most economically bought in the shell and should be refrigerated or frozen once the shell is removed.

Dried fruit—raisins, dates, figs, apples, apricots, currants, etc.— add much flavor and color to yeast and quick breads, cookies, and cakes. These chopped fruits can be substituted, measure for measure, for candied fruit and citron without losing the colorfulness of the product. Sun-dried or honey-dipped fruits are preferred to oven-dried and sulphur-preserved ones.

Fresh fruit and vegetables should not be ignored. Grated citrus rinds of lemons, limes, oranges, grapefruit, and tangerines can break the monotony of vanilla extract. Substitute fresh fruit, carrot, or tomato juice for water. Fresh or frozen cranberries are excellent for use in baking. The berries are firm and crisp and retain their shape and texture well in baking.

Vanilla extract should be made from vanilla, alcohol, and water only. Artificial imitation vanilla is a chemically synthesized product.

Carob powder, or flour, is ground from St. John's Bread, or the pods of the tropical tree *ceratonia siliqua*. It is most commonly used as a chocolate substitute since it does not contain any of the undesirable substances found in chocolate, yet tastes very much like it. Only a couple of tablespoons are usually necessary to obtain the chocolate-like flavor. A larger amount of carob powder tends to make a very heavy product. Untoasted and toasted carob powders may be used interchangeably, although toasted carob powder tastes more like chocolate. A low baking temperature, 300-325° F., should be used since carob burns at moderate to high temperatures. If desired, chocolate powder may be substituted in the ratio of two measures of chocolate powder to one measure of carob.

Nutritional Supplements

There are a number of nutritional supplements which may be added to baked goods with little or no change in taste. These supplements are added in small quantities and have little effect on the proportions of other ingredients, although an additional teaspoonful of liquid may be added for each tablespoon of supplement.

Two or three tablespoons of wheat germ or bran flakes can add a slightly nutty flavor and texture to a baked product. Wheat germ and bran are particularly high in B vitamins, protein, and minerals. In addition, the germ is an excellent source of vitamin E. They can be used in breads, rolls, cakes, and cookies.

Soy flour, either high fat or low fat, is an excellent source of protein. Soy flour is ground from soybeans which are the only vegetable source of complete protein in that they contain all the amino acids essential to man. Other vegetable proteins are incomplete; that is, they do not contain all of the essential amino acids. Several tablespoons of soy flour may be added to breads, rolls, and cookies.

Several tablespoons of non-instant milk powder (whole or skim) produce a richer product, not only in taste, but in calcium, minerals and proteins. Instant milk powders may also be used, but they contain a lower protein content. Milk powders may be used in breads, rolls, cookies, cakes, pies, and puddings.

Only a little kelp powder (about 1 teaspoon) should be added to avoid possible off-colors in breads, rolls, and cookies. It is a good source of minerals, particularly iodine.

Brewer's yeast has been previously discussed as an excellent source of B vitamins. Because it may leave a bitter taste, use sparingly—about 2-3 teaspoons in breads, rolls, and cookies.

BREADBAKING TECHNIQUES

Combining Ingredients

The yeast is usually prepared first by dissolving it in warm water or milk. The warm liquid should be no hotter than 110° F. if the yeasts are to remain viable. If a juice or yogurt is used as the liquid, the yeast should be dissolved in about 1/4 cup warm water before being added to the juice. Sourdough starters, which contain yeast, are prepared the night before or at least 10 hours in advance.

The sweetening, salt, and all other ingredients except flour, fruit, and nuts are stirred in. Flour is slowly added and stirred. When the dough leaves the side of the bowl, no additional flour is required, and the dough is ready to be kneaded. Because the amount of flour added to the dough may vary every time bread is made, it is more important to rely on the condition of the dough rather than the number of cups to signal when enough flour has been added. If there are fruit and nuts in the recipe, they are added just before kneading.

Kneading

Before turning the dough out from the bowl, lightly flour the surface on which the dough will be kneaded. A wooden board about 18 inches square is easiest to work on, but a counter or table top will suffice.

Turn the dough out on the floured surface and sprinkle a little flour over it to keep it from sticking to the fingers. It may be necessary to sprinkle flour over the board and dough several times again before the stickiness disappears. The stickiness is slowly lost as the dough is kneaded. Kneading develops the gluten which ensures that the dough will trap the gas given off by the yeast. The longer the dough is kneaded and the better the glutens develop, the finer the bread will be. A poorly kneaded loaf has many large holes, while a well kneaded loaf has small, uniform holes.

The dough is kneaded by a downward and forward motion with the heels of the hands. With the fingers, bring the far end of the dough forward, then press hard downward and push away with the heels of the hands. Repeat. Turn the dough slightly, fold it back in again, and push down and away. With practice, this will become a natural and rythmic process. Continue kneading for about five to ten minutes or until the dough is no longer sticky, but smooth, satiny, and elastic. At this point, the dough begins to take on a "life" of its own. Press it with a finger and it springs back. Stretch it and it snaps back.

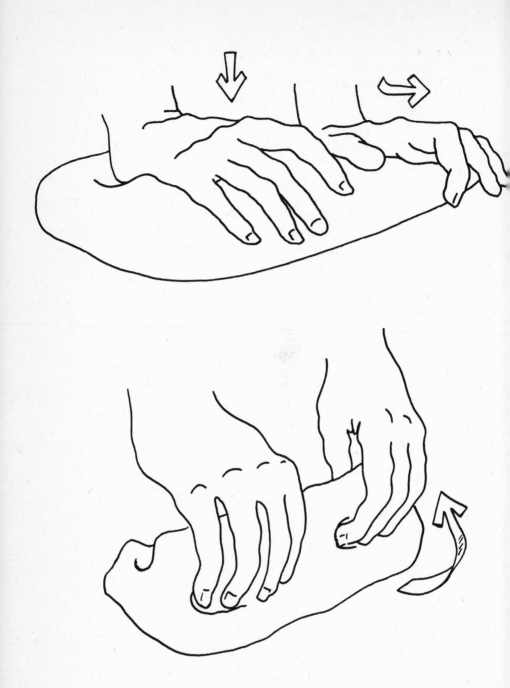

Kneading dough.

Many recipes instruct to knead the dough once, let it rise, then knead it again. The purpose of the first kneading is to develop the gluten. The second kneading ensures that the bread will have a finer grain than would be obtained if it were only kneaded once. For this reason, the second kneading can be skipped altogether. The only difference in the final product will be a slightly coarser grain. If the dough is kneaded a second time, only a few minutes of kneading is necessary. Although most of the recipes in this book specify only one rising, all of them may be risen twice.

Rising or Proofing

If two risings are preferred, the kneaded dough should be shaped into a ball and placed in a well-greased bowl. Roll the dough around in the bowl to coat its entire surface with oil to prevent the dough from drying. Cover the bowl with a clean dish cloth and set it in a warm place to rise, or proof. A temperature range of 80-85° F. is considered ideal. A damp, not wet, dishcloth may also be used over the oiled dough to ensure against drying and the formation of a crust. If the room is drafty, it should be placed in a sheltered spot such as an unused cabinet or the unheated oven. In cool weather, placing the bowl in a pan of warm water (about 110° F.) will help to provide the correct temperature. The dough should be allowed to rise until it has doubled in bulk. The rising time is dependent on the temperature—at 70° F., it may take 1 1/2-2 hours, but at 85° F., it may require only 30 minutes. It is usually better to check the dough occasionally rather than to rely on a timer.

When the dough has doubled in bulk, punch it down by pushing a closed fist into the proofed dough. Turn the dough out on a very lightly floured board and knead gently for a few minutes.

Shaping

If a double recipe or recipe for 2 loaves is used, divide the dough into one-loaf parts. The dough may be shaped by first rolling it out into a circle about 9 inches in diameter (for a large loaf), then folding the sides in and pinching the seams together. The dough is then turned upside down and placed in the greased loaf pan. This will make the typical loaf which rises in the center. The same effect can also be achieved by gently kneading the dough into shape.

Most of the recipes specify large loaf pans, but round pans, square pans, or no pans may be used. French or Italian breads are rolled into long loaves and placed on a greased cookie sheet sprinkled with cornmeal. Other shapes—circles, knots, braids, etc.—are also baked on cookie sheets. When baking breads without pans having sides, the dough should be relatively stiff. A dough that is not stiff enough will not support the bulk and will only grow sideways instead of upwards.

Decorating

Decorating is an optional step, but perhaps the most fun because of the unlimited possibilities and no strict rules to follow. It should be done after shaping and before the final rising.

Cutting patterns into the top of the dough should be done with a thin, very sharp knife. Cuts should be made no more than 1/8 inch deep and may be of anything—lines, geometric patterns, initials, bread art, etc. Very simple designs are usually most successful, especially since the rising dough may not open the cuts evenly.

Shaping dough for loaf pans.

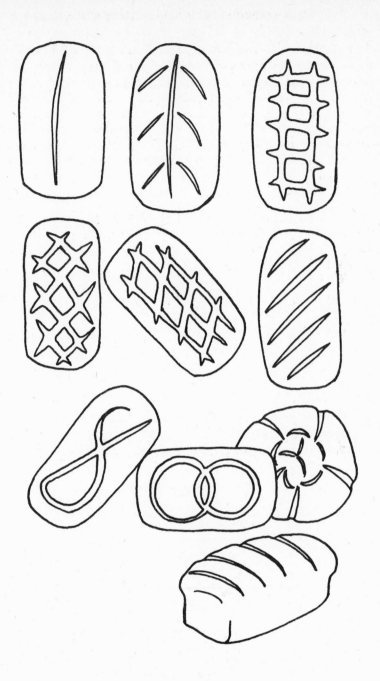

Decorative cutting on breads.

A glaze may be applied after cutting. There are several common glazes that give a rich, golden brown crust. An egg yolk glaze is made by stirring one egg yolk with 1 tablespoon milk or cream. A similar glaze is made with a whole egg, well beaten, mixed with 1 tablespoon water or cream. The cream glaze is simply a light or medium cream. Glazes are lightly brushed on the dough with a pastry brush. Only a thin film of glaze is needed.

The loaf can now be sprinkled with sesame or poppy seeds or chopped nuts or dried fruit. To ensure that the topping adheres to the loaf, use the fingers to press it gently into the loaf.

Final Rising

The same rules are followed for both the first and final rising. The dough should be covered with a dish cloth and set in a warm place until double in bulk, or until it has risen about 3/4 inch above the rim of the loaf pan. It will rise a little more in the oven.

Should the dough over-proof or rise too much during this rising, it is best to punch it down, reshape it, and allow it to rise again. Overproofing usually indicates that there may be a tunnel through the loaf and that the holes may be large, resulting in a somewhat coarse bread.

Baking

The oven should be preheated, usually to 350° F. Bake the bread until it pulls away from the pan, coming out of the pan easily when dumped upside down. Baking usually takes between 45 and 60 minutes.

When bread is removed from the oven, it should be removed from the pan immediately and allowed to cool on cookie racks.

Storage

Bread may be kept at room temperature wrapped in plastic for about a week during the winter, but molds attack it after only a few days in the summer. If it must be stored for long periods, seal it well in an airtight plastic bag and store it in the refrigerator or freezer. While all refrigerators and freezers tend to dry bread out somewhat, frost-free models are the worst offenders.

Frozen breads may be reheated by wrapping them in aluminum foil and placing them in a low oven until they are warm.

CONVERTING CONVENTIONAL RECIPES TO WHOLE GRAINS AND ORGANIC INGREDIENTS

Even if one enjoys whole grains and organic ingredients, there is no reason why other recipes and cookbooks should be discarded or ignored. Favorite family recipes or exciting new ones can be easily converted to using whole grains and organic ingredients.

Most ingredients can be converted measure for measure, but some are a bit tricky. The compactness of flour creates variations in its precise quantity, but it can usually be used cup for cup. The following is a summary of common conversions from ordinary recipes.

Processed Ingredients	Natural Ingredients
1 pkg. dry yeast	1 T. dry yeast
1 c. white flour	1 c. whole wheat flour
1 c. white sugar	1 c. raw sugar, or
	1/2 - 3/4 c. honey, or
	3/4 c. molasses
1 c. salted butter	1 c. sweet butter plus
	1 t. salt
1 c. margarine	1 c. sweet butter plus
	1 t. salt
1 c. shortening	1 c. sweet butter, or
	1 c. lard
1 t. vanilla	1 t. pure vanilla extract, or
	2 t. grated lemon rind plus
	1 t. lemon juice
1 c. candied fruit	1 c. chopped cranberries,
	citrus rinds, and dried
	fruit

CHAPTER 3

THE BASIC RECIPES
FOR YEAST BREADS

THE PRECEDING CHAPTER discussed the ingredients and techniques used in bread baking. This chapter contains 26 recipes for yeast breads. It is not meant as a complete and final collection of whole grain yeast bread recipes, but rather as a basic foundation for baking a limitless variety of breads.

BASIC WHOLE WHEAT BREAD I
(two large loaves)

1 T. dry yeast	2 t. salt
3 1/2 c. warm water	8-9 c. whole wheat flour
2 T. raw sugar	

Grease two large loaf pans (9″ x 5″ x 2 3/4″).

Pour the water into a large mixing bowl and sprinkle the yeast over it. Allow the yeast to dissolve, about 5 minutes. Add the sugar, salt, and about 4 cups of flour. Stir well. Continue stirring and adding flour, a little at a time, until the dough becomes stiff and pulls away from the side of the bowl.

Turn the dough out on a floured board and knead for 5-7 minutes or until the dough is smooth and elastic.

Divide the dough into two equal parts, shape, and place in bread pans. Cover with a clean dish towel and allow to rise in a warm spot until about double in bulk.

Preheat the oven to 350° F.

Bake for 40-45 minutes or until done.

BASIC WHOLE WHEAT BREAD II
(one large loaf)

1 1/2 t. dry yeast	2 T. skim milk powder
1 3/4 c. warm water	1 T. Liquid oil
1 1/2 T. molasses	4 - 4 1/2 c. whole wheat flour
1 t. salt	

Grease one large bread pan (9″ x 5″ 2 3/4″).

Pour the water into a large mixing bowl and sprinkle the yeast over it. Allow the yeast to dissolve, about 5 minutes. Add the molasses, salt, milk powder, oil, and about 2 cups of flour. Stir well. Continue stirring and adding a little flour at a time until the dough becomes stiff and pulls away from the side of the bowl.

Turn the dough out on a floured board and knead for 5-7 minutes or until the dough is smooth and elastic.

Shape the dough and place it in the bread pan. Cover it with a clean dish cloth and allow it to rise in a warm spot until about double in bulk.

Preheat the oven to 350° F.

Bake for 45-50 minutes or until done.

WHEAT GERM BREAD
(two large loaves)

1 T. dry yeast	2 t. salt
3 1/2 c. warm water	1 c. wheat germ
2 T. molasses	7 1/2 - 8 1/2 c. whole wheat
	flour

Grease two large bread pans (9″ x 5″ x 2 3/4″).

Sprinkle the yeast over the warm water in a large mixing bowl. Allow the yeast to dissolve, about 5 minutes. Add the molasses, wheat germ, and salt. Stir well. Add 4 cups of flour and stir. Slowly continue adding flour until the dough becomes stiff and pulls away from the sides of the mixing bowl.

Turn the dough out onto a floured board and knead for 5-7 minutes or until the dough is smooth and elastic.

Divide the dough into two equal parts, shape, and place in bread pans. Cover with a clean dish towel and allow to rise in a warm spot until about double in bulk.

Preheat the oven to 350° F.

Bake for 50 minutes or until done.

RYE BREAD
(two large loaves)

1 T. dry yeast	2 t. salt
3 1/2 c. warm water	2 T. liquid oil
3 T. milk powder	3 c. whole wheat flour
2 T. raw sugar	6-7 c. whole rye flour

Grease two large bread pans (9" x 5" x 2 3/4").

Pour the water into a large mixing bowl and sprinkle the yeast over it. Allow the yeast to dissolve, about 5 minutes. Stir in the milk powder, sugar, salt, oil, and whole wheat flour. Slowly add the rye flour and stir until the dough becomes stiff and pulls away from the sides of the mixing bowl.

Turn the dough out on a floured board and knead for 5-7 minutes or until the dough is smooth and elastic.

Divide the dough into two equal parts, shape, and place in the bread pans. Brush the tops with liquid oil and cover with a clean dish cloth. Allow the bread to rise in a warm spot until the top of the dough has risen to about 1/2 to 3/4 inch above the rim of the pan.

Preheat the oven to 350° F.

Bake for 50 minutes or until done.

BRAN BREAD
(one large loaf)

1 1/2 t. dry yeast	1/4 c. milk powder
1 3/4 c. warm water	1 T. liquid oil
2 T. molasses	1 c. bran flakes
1 t. salt	4 - 4 1/2 c. whole wheat flour

Grease one large bread pan (9" x 5" x 2 3/4").

Sprinkle the yeast over the warm water in a large mixing bowl. Allow the yeast to dissolve, about 5 minutes. Add the molasses, salt, milk powder, oil, and bran flakes. Slowly add the flour until the dough stiffens and pulls away from the side of the bowl.

Turn the dough out on a floured board and knead for 5-7 minutes or until the dough is smooth and elastic.

Shape the dough and place in the greased pan. Cover with a clean dish cloth and place in a warm spot to rise until about double in bulk.

Preheat the oven to 350° F.

Brush the top of the loaf with cream or liquid oil. Bake for 45-50 minutes or until done.

GRIT WHEAT BREAD
(two large loaves)

1 c. corn grits	2 T. molasses
1 1/2 c. water	2 t. salt
1 T. dry yeast	2 T. liquid oil
1 1/2 c. warm water	8-9 c. whole wheat flour

Combine the grits and 1 1/2 c. water in a saucepan, bring to a boil and simmer slowly for 5 minutes. Allow to cool until lukewarm.

Grease two large bread pans (9" x 5" x 2 3/4").

Add the yeast and 1 1/2 cups warm water to a large mixing bowl. Allow the yeast to dissolve, about 5 minutes. Stir in the molasses, salt, oil, and grits. Add 4 cups of flour and stir. Slowly add the remaining flour until the dough pulls away from the side of the bowl.

Turn the dough out on a lightly floured board and knead until it feels smooth and elastic, about 5-7 minutes.

Divide the dough into two equal parts, shape, and place in the greased pans. Cover with a clean dish cloth and set in a warm place to rise until double in bulk.

Preheat the oven to 350° F.

Bake for 50 minutes or until done.

SOY BREAD
(one large loaf)

1 1/2 t. dry yeast	1 t. salt
1 3/4 c. warm water	1 c. soy flour
1 T. molasses	3 1/2 - 4 c. whole wheat flour

Grease one large bread pan (9″ x 5″ x 2 3/4″).

Sprinkle the yeast over the water in a large mixing bowl. Allow the yeast to dissolve, about 5 minutes. Stir in the molasses, salt, and soy flour. Slowly add the wheat flour until the dough stiffens and pulls away from the side of the bowl.

Turn the dough out on a lightly floured board and knead until the dough feels smooth and elastic, about 5-7 minutes.

Shape the dough and place it in the greased pan. Cover with a clean dish cloth and set in a warm place to rise. Allow the dough to rise until it is about 1/2 inch above the rim of the bread pan.

Preheat the oven to 325° F.

Bake for 50-60 minutes or until done.

RAISIN BREAD
(two large loaves)

1 T. dry yeast	2 T. liquid oil
3 1/2 c. warm water	1 T. cinnamon
3 T. molasses	1/2 t. powdered ginger
2 t. salt	1 c. raisins
3 T. milk powder	9-10 c. whole wheat flour

Grease two large bread pans (9″ x 5″ x 2 3/4″).

Sprinkle the yeast over the warm water in a large mixing bowl. Allow the yeast to dissolve, about 5 minutes. Add the molasses, salt, milk powder, oil, cinnamon, ginger, raisins, and 4 cups of flour. Stir well. Continue to add the flour, a little at a time, until the dough becomes stiff and pulls away from the sides of the mixing bowl.

Turn the dough out onto a floured board and knead for 5-7 minutes or until the dough is smooth and elastic.

Divide the dough into two equal parts, shape, and place in the bread pans. Cover with a clean dish cloth and allow to rise in a warm spot until about double in bulk.

Preheat the oven to 350° F.
Bake for 50 minutes or until done.

OATMEAL BREAD
(one large loaf)

1 1/2 t. dry yeast	1/4 c. milk powder
2 c. warm water	3/4 c. rolled oats, uncooked
1 T. molasses	1 T. liquid oil
1 t. salt	4 1/2 - 5 c. whole wheat flour

Grease one large bread pan (9" x 5" x 2 3/4").

Pour the water into a large mixing bowl and sprinkle the yeast over it. Allow the yeast to dissolve, about 5 minutes. Add the molasses, salt, milk powder, oats, and liquid oil. Stir. Slowly add the flour until the dough stiffens and pulls away from the side of the bowl.

Turn the dough out on a floured board and knead for 5-7 minutes or until the dough is smooth and elastic and is no longer sticky.

Shape the dough and place it in the bread pan. Brush the top with liquid oil and cover with a clean dish cloth. Place the bread to rise in a warm spot until about double in bulk.

Preheat the oven to 350° F.

Bake for 50 minutes or until done.

YOGURT BREAD
(two large loaves)

1 T. dry yeast	2 t. salt
2 c. warm water	1 1/2 c. rye flour
2 T. honey	7-9 c. whole wheat flour
1 c. yogurt, plain	

Grease two large bread pans (9" x 5" x 2 3/4").

Add the water and the yeast to a large mixing bowl. Allow the yeast to dissolve, about 5 minutes. Stir in the honey, yogurt, salt, and rye flour. Slowly add the wheat flour until the dough pulls away from the side of the bowl.

Turn the dough out on a floured board and knead until it feels smooth and elastic, about 5-7 minutes.

Divide the dough into two equal parts, shape, and place in the greased pans. Cover with a clean dish cloth and set in a warm place to rise. Allow the dough to rise until it is 1/2-3/4 inch above the rim of the pan.

Preheat the oven to 350° F.

Bake for 45-50 minutes or until done.

(*Note:* Yogurt bread has its own unique flavor—sour, yet distinctively different from sourdough bread, since a different fermentation process is involved. Its taste grows stronger with a longer rising period, so the single rising method is preferred.)

RICH EGG BREAD
(one large loaf)

1 1/2 t. dry yeast	2 T. milk powder
1 c. warm water	1 T. liquid oil
2 T. honey	2 eggs, beaten
1 t. salt	4 1/2 - 5 c. whole wheat flour

Grease one large bread pan (9" x 5" x 2 3/4").

Sprinkle the yeast over the water in a large mixing bowl. Allow the yeast to dissolve, about 5 minutes. Stir in the honey, salt, milk powder, oil, and eggs. Slowly add the flour until the dough pulls away from the sides of the mixing bowl.

Turn the dough out on a lightly floured board and knead for 5-7 minutes or until the dough is smooth and elastic.

Shape the dough and place it in the baking pan. Cover it with a clean dish cloth and set it in a warm place to rise until it has doubled in bulk.

Preheat the oven to 350° F.

Bursh the top of the loaf with cream or a beaten egg. Bake for 45 minutes or until done.

BATTER BREAD
(one large loaf)

1 1/2 t. dry yeast	1 T. liquid oil
1 3/4 c. warm water	1 c. coarse bran flakes
2 T. raw sugar	3 1/2 c. whole wheat flour
1 t. salt	

Grease one large bread pan (9" x 5" x 2 3/4").

Pour the water into a large mixing bowl and sprinkle yeast over it. Allow the yeast to dissolve, about 5 minutes. Stir in the sugar, salt, oil, and bran. Slowly stir in the flour until the dough begins to stiffen. The dough should be soft enough to beat with a wooden spoon. Beat the dough vigorously for about 5 minutes.

Cover the bowl with a clean dish cloth and allow to rise in a warm place until double in bulk.

Stir the batter down and beat vigorously again. Pour into the loaf pan, cover with a dish cloth, and allow to rise again until double in bulk.

Preheat the oven to 350° F.

Bake for 45 minutes or until done.

ANADAMA BREAD
(two large loaves)

1/2 c. cornmeal	3 T. butter
1 c. milk	1/2 c. molasses
1 T. dry yeast	1 t. salt
1 1/2 c. water	6-7 c. whole wheat flour

Grease two large bread pans (9" x 5" x 2 3/4").

In a small bowl, sprinkle yeast over 1/4 cup milk.

In a 4 quart saucepan, combine the water, cornmeal, and 3/4 cup milk. Stir over low heat, and remove from heat before the mixture comes to a boil. Add the butter, molasses, and salt. Allow to cool.

When the liquid has cooled to lukewarm, pour into a large bowl and add the yeast. Slowly stir in the flour until the dough pulls away from the side of the bowl.

Turn the dough out on a floured board and knead until it feels smooth and elastic, about 5-7 minutes.

Divide the dough into two equal parts, shape, and place in the greased pans. Cover with a clean dish cloth and set in a warm place to rise until about double in bulk.

Preheat the oven to 350° F.

Bake for 50 minutes or until done.

BROWN RICE BREAD
(one large loaf)

1 1/2 t. dry yeast	3 T. skim milk powder
1 3/4 c. warm water	2 c. brown rice,
1 T. molasses	cooked and cooled
1 t. salt	3 1/2 - 4 1/2 c. whole wheat
3 T. liquid oil	flour

Grease one large bread pan (9" x 5" x 2 3/4").

In a large mixing bowl, combine the yeast and water and allow the yeast to dissolve, about 5 minutes. Stir in the molasses, salt, oil, milk powder, and rice. Slowly add the flour until the dough begins to pull away from the side of the bowl.

Turn the dough out on a floured board and knead until it is smooth and elastic, about 5-7 minutes.

Shape the dough and place it in the greased pan. Cover with a clean dish cloth and set in a warm place to rise until about double in bulk.

Preheat the oven to 350° F.

Brush the top of the loaf with a glaze, if desired. Bake for 50 minutes or until done.

BARLEY BREAD
(one large loaf)

1 1/2 t. dry yeast	1 T. liquid oil
1 3/4 c. warm water	3 T. wheat germ
1 T. raw sugar	1 c. barley flour
1 t. salt	3 1/2 - 4 c. whole wheat flour

Grease one large loaf pan (9″ x 5″ x 2 3/4″).

Sprinkle the yeast over the warm water in a large mixing bowl. Allow the yeast to dissolve, about 5 minutes. Stir in the sugar, salt, oil, wheat germ, and barley flour. Slowly add the whole wheat flour until the dough stiffens and no longer sticks to the side of the bowl.

Turn the dough out on a lightly floured board and knead until the dough feels elastic, about 5-7 minutes.

Shape the dough and place it in the greased pan. Brush liquid oil over the top of the loaf. Cover with a clean dish cloth and set in a warm place to rise until double in bulk.

Preheat the oven to 350° F.

Bake for 50 minutes or until done.

MILLET BREAD
(one large loaf)

1 1/2 t. dry yeast	3 T. milk powder
1 3/4 c. warm water	1 t. salt
2 T. raw sugar	1 c. millet meal
1 T. liquid oil	3 1/2 - 4 c. whole wheat flour

Grease one large bread pan (9" x 5" x 2 3/4").

Sprinkle yeast over the water in a large mixing bowl. Allow the yeast to dissolve, about 5 minutes. Stir in the sugar, oil, milk powder, salt, and millet meal. Slowly add the flour until the dough stiffens and pulls away from the side of the bowl.

Turn the dough out on a floured board and knead until it feels smooth and elastic, about 5-7 minutes.

Shape the dough and place it in the bread pan. Brush with liquid oil, cover with a clean dish cloth and place in a warm place. Allow the dough to rise until about double in bulk.

Preheat the oven to 350° F.

Bake for 45-50 minutes or until done.

BUCKWHEAT BREAD
(one large loaf)

1 1/2 t. dry yeast	3 T. milk powder
1 3/4 c. warm water	1 1/2 c. buckwheat flour
2 T. raw sugar	3 - 3 1/2 c. whole wheat flour
1 t. salt	

Grease one large loaf pan (9" x 5" x 2 3/4").

Sprinkle the yeast over the water in a large mixing bowl. Allow the yeast to dissolve, about 5-7 minutes. Stir in the sugar, salt, milk powder, and buckwheat flour. Slowly add the wheat flour until the dough stiffens and pulls away from the side of the bowl.

Turn the dough out on a floured board and knead until it feels elastic, about 5-7 minutes.

Shape the dough and place it in the greased pan. Cover it with a clean dish cloth and set in a warm place to rise until about double in bulk.

Preheat the oven to 350° F.

Bake for 50-60 minutes or until done.

PEANUT BREAD
(one large loaf)

2 t. dry yeast	1/4 c. milk powder
1 3/4 c. warm water	1 1/2 c. peanut flour,
3 T. raw sugar	raw or toasted
1 1/2 t. salt	4 1/2 - 5 c. whole wheat flour

Grease one large loaf pan (9" x 5" x 2 3/4").

Sprinkle the yeast over the water in a large mixing bowl. Allow the yeast to dissolve, about 5 minutes. Stir in the sugar, salt, milk powder, and peanut flour. Slowly add the wheat flour until the dough stiffens and no longer sticks to the side of the bowl.

Turn the dough out on a floured board and knead until the dough feels elastic or springs back at the touch, about 5-7 minutes.

Shape the dough and place in the pan. Cover with a clean dish cloth, set in a warm place, and allow to rise until about double in bulk.

Preheat the oven to 350° F.

Bake for 50-60 minutes or until done.

TOMATO BREAD
(one large loaf)

2 t. dry yeast	1/2 t. salt
1/4 c. warm water	1 T. liquid oil
1 1/2 c. tomato juice	1/2 t. basil, powdered
1 T. raw sugar	4 1/2 - 5 c. whole wheat flour

Grease one large bread pan (9" x 5" x 2 3/4").

Pour the water over the yeast in a large mixing bowl. Allow the yeast to dissolve, about 5 minutes. Stir in the tomato juice, raw sugar, salt, oil, and basil. Slowly add the flour until the dough stiffens and no longer sticks to the side of the bowl.

Turn the dough out onto a floured board and knead until the dough feels smooth and elastic, or about 5-7 minutes.

Shape the dough and place it in the pan. Cover with a clean dish cloth and allow to rise until about double in bulk.

Preheat the oven to 350° F.

Bake for 50-60 minutes or until done.

PUMPKIN BREAD
(one large loaf)

1 T. dry yeast	1 T. bran flakes
1 c. warm milk	1/2 t. cinnamon
2 T. sugar	1/4 t. ginger, powdered
1 egg, beaten	dash of nutmeg
1 t. salt	3 1/2 - 4 1/2 c. whole wheat
1/2 c. pumpkin pureé	flour
2 T. liquid oil	1 egg, well beaten
3 T. milk powder	(for glaze)

Grease one large loaf pan (9" x 5" x 2 3/4").

Sprinkle the yeast over the warm milk in a large mixing bowl. Allow the yeast to dissolve, about 5 minutes. Add the sugar, egg, salt, pumpkin pureé, oil, milk powder, bran flakes, cinnamon, ginger, and nutmeg. Slowly stir in the flour until the dough stiffens and pulls away from the side of the bowl.

Turn the dough out on a floured board and knead until it feels smooth and elastic, about 5-7 minutes.

Shape the dough and place it in the loaf pan. Brush lightly with the beaten egg. Cover with a clean dish cloth and set in a warm place. Allow the dough to rise until it has about doubled in bulk, or until the dough has risen to about 3/4 inch above the rim of the pan.

Preheat the oven to 350° F.

Bake for 50-60 minutes or until done.

CAROB BREAD
(one large loaf)

2 t. dry yeast	3 T. skim milk powder
1 3/4 c. warm water	2 T. liquid oil
3 T. molasses	3 T. carob powder, toasted
1 t. salt	4 1/2 - 5 c. whole wheat flour

Grease one large loaf pan (9" x 5" x 2 3/4").

In a large mixing bowl, combine the yeast and water and allow the yeast to dissolve, about 5 minutes. Add the molasses, salt, milk powder, oil, and carob, and stir well. Slowly add the flour until the dough pulls away from the side of the bowl.

Turn the dough out on a lightly floured board and knead until it feels smooth and elastic, about 5-7 minutes.

Shape the dough and place in the greased pan. Cover the loaf with a clean dish cloth and set in a warm place to rise. Allow the dough to rise until it is about 1/2-3/4 inch above the rim of the pan.

Preheat the oven to 325° F.

Bake for 50-60 minutes or until done. To prevent the top of the loaf from burning, brush with water 2 or 3 times during baking.

CRANBERRY BREAD
(two large loaves)

1 T. dry yeast	2 T. butter, melted
3 c. warm water	8-9 c. whole wheat flour
1/2 c. raw sugar	3/4 c. nuts, chopped
3 T. honey	2 c. cranberries, fresh or
2 t. salt	frozen, coarsely chopped
3 T. milk powder	

Grease two large bread pans (9" x 5" x 2 3/4").

Pour the water into a large mixing bowl and sprinkle yeast over it. Allow the yeast to dissolve, about 5 minutes. Stir in the sugar, honey, salt, milk powder, and butter. Add the flour, a little at a time, until the dough stiffens and pulls away from the side of the bowl. Stir in the nuts and cranberries.

Turn the dough out on a floured board and knead for 5-7 minutes or until the dough is smooth and elastic.

Divide the dough into two equal parts, shape, and place in the bread pans. Cover with a clean dish cloth and allow to rise in a warm spot until about double in bulk.

Preheat the oven to 350° F.

Brush a glaze over the top of the loaf, if desired. Bake for 45-50 minutes or until done.

SWEET BREAD
(two large loaves)

1/2 c. scalded milk	2 T. butter, melted and cooled
2 T. dry yeast	1 1/2 c. raw sugar
2/3 c. warm water	1 t. salt
5 eggs, slightly beaten	8-10 c. whole wheat flour
2 t. grated lemon rind	1 egg, beaten (for glaze)

Grease two large bread pans (9" x 5" x 2 3/4").

Scald the milk.

Sprinkle the yeast over the water in a large mixing bowl. Allow the yeast to dissolve, about 5 minutes. Stir in the milk, eggs, lemon rind, butter, sugar, salt, and about 4 cups of flour. Slowly add the remaining flour until the dough stiffens.

Turn the dough out on a floured board and knead, sprinkling additional flour over the dough to keep it from sticking. Knead for about 10 minutes, or until the dough no longer sticks to your hands.

Divide the dough into two equal parts, shape, and place in bread pans. Cover with a clean dish cloth and let rise until double in bulk.

Preheat the oven to 325° F.

Brush the tops of the loaves with the well-beaten egg. Bake for 50 minutes to 1 hour or until done.

ARABIC BREAD
(about 12 loaves)

2 T. dry yeast   1 T. sugar
2 c. warm water   6 c. whole wheat flour
1 t. salt

Preheat the oven to 475° F. Grease two cookie sheets.

Pour the water into a large mixing bowl and sprinkle the yeast over it. Allow the yeast to dissolve, about 5 minutes. Add the salt and sugar. Slowly add the flour until the dough stiffens and begins to pull away from the side of the bowl.

Turn the dough out on a lightly floured board and knead for about 5-8 minutes or until the dough feels elastic.

Divide the dough into about 12 equal parts. Shape each part into a ball, then roll out each ball into a circle about 6 inches in diameter.

Place on the cookie sheets and bake for 10-12 minutes or until lightly browned. They must be carefully watched since they burn very easily.

STEAMED BROWN BREAD
(one large loaf)

1 T. dry yeast	3 T. skim milk powder
1 c. warm water	1/2 c. cornmeal
1/3 c. molasses	4 - 4 1/2 c. whole wheat flour
1/2 t. salt	

In a large mixing bowl, combine the yeast and warm water and allow the yeast to dissolve, about 5 minutes. Add the molasses, salt, milk powder, and cornmeal. Slowly add the flour until the dough just begins to pull away from the side of the bowl. The dough should be fairly soft and not as stiff as bread dough that is baked.

Turn the dough out on a floured board, and knead until it is smooth and elastic.

Shape the dough and place it in a greased large loaf pan (9″ x 5″ x 2 3/4″), or divide the dough into two parts, shape, and place in two #303 cans (16 ounces).

Heat the water in a steamer with a tight lid. At the start, the water should be almost as high as the steaming rack, but not touching the rack. Bring the water to a rolling boil.

Carefully place the bread pan or cans on the steaming rack. The dough should not be allowed to double in bulk, although it may be allowed to rest for about 15 minutes prior to steaming.

Cover the steamer and steam for about 40 minutes over water at a medium boil.

DIM SUM (CHINESE FILLED BUNS)
(about 18 buns)

1 T. dry yeast	1 t. salt
1/4 c. warm water	1/3 c. raw sugar
1 1/2 c. hot water	6-7 c. whole wheat flour
1 1/2 T. lard	

Filling:

1 1/2 lb. roast pork, cooked
   and cut into 3/8" cubes
1/2 c. mushrooms, chopped
1/2 c. water chestnuts,
   chopped (optional)

3 stalks scallions, minced
1/4 c. soy sauce
1 T. raw sugar
1/2 t. ginger, powdered
sprinkle of garlic

In a small mixing bowl or cup, combine the yeast with 1/4 cup warm water. Set aside to allow the yeast to dissolve.

In a large mixing bowl, combine the hot water, lard, salt, and sugar. Stir until all ingredients have dissolved. Allow this mixture to cool until it is lukewarm. Stir in the yeast paste. Slowly add the flour until

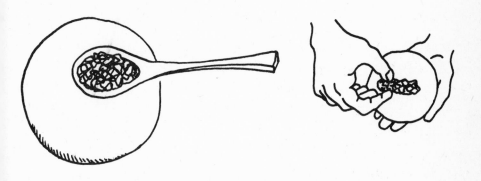

Making Dim Sum.

the dough pulls away from the side of the bowl. Cover the bowl with a clean dish cloth and set it in a warm place to rise until about double in bulk. It is not necessary to knead the dough.

Prepare the filling while the dough is rising. Heat all of the filling ingredients except the scallions in a large skillet or saucepan. Stir and cook until most of the moisture has been absorbed. Remove from the heat and add the scallions. Allow the filling to cool.

Cut a few sheets of white paper into squares 2 1/2" x 2 1/2".

When the dough has doubled in bulk, punch it down and turn it out on a floured board. Knead the dough until smooth and elastic. This dough should be fairly soft, not as stiff as bread dough.

Divide the dough into about 18 equal parts. Shape each part into a ball. Roll out each ball into a circle about 1/4" thick. Place a tablespoon of filling in the center of each. Bring the edges of the dough together, pinching them to seal the bun. Place the bun, seam-side down, on a square piece of paper.

Bring the water in the steamer to a boil. Carefully place the buns with paper on the steaming rack and steam for 15 minutes. Dim Sum is best served hot.

(*Note:* Fillings of other meats and vegetables may also be used.)

CHAPTER 4

BAKING
WITH SOURDOUGH STARTERS

IN THE MINDS of many, sourdough bread is a mysterious commodity which brings nostalgic recollections of San Francisco or Paris. Although Greensboro or Chicago sourdough bread may not sound quite as exciting, it can be just as good, or better. Sourdough introduces a new dimension of bread taste—sourness. There is absolutely nothing mysterious or exotic about making sourdough bread. In fact, by using starter to make sourdough bread, it is possible to save yeast money on every loaf baked.

SOURDOUGH STARTER

When our nation was younger, and men ventured beyond the reaches of the corner grocery store, miners and trappers of the Far West and Northwest always carried a pot of sourdough starter with them. Being far from fresh provisions, they either had to settle for hard, stale biscuits or had to make their own fresh bread. Fresh yeast spoils easily when not refrigerated; sourdough starter freshened often was the answer. Thus their nickname of "Sourdoughs." Without their precious sourdough starter and the light pancakes, tangy biscuits, and aromatic bread it made possible, meals would have been dull.

Starter is the essence of sourdough bread. The sourdough starter contains an everlasting supply of yeast. It provides yeast for the first loaf of sourdough bread, and the next, and the next, and infinitely ever after. The starter is simply the "seed yeast" and the medium in which it lives. The only requirement for the medium is that it be something hospitable to yeast and compatible with bread, i.e., a starchy food. Any of a number of starchy foods can be used—wheat, rye, cornmeal, potatoes, or rice. Whole wheat flour is the best. It is always available, requires no preparation—as do potatoes and rice— and is an important ingredient in every loaf of bread. It is possible, however, to use a variety of different starters for different kinds of bread. This collection of starters will keep the refrigerator well stocked, but will make very little difference in the bread which is baked. For example, pumpernickel bread made with potato starter tastes no different from pumpernickel bread made with wheat starter. Because of this it is only necessary to maintain one pot of starter.

Starter has to be "started" sometime—whether it's a portion of precious 14-year old starter from an old sourdough or one made in the kitchen today. To make starter, combine 1/4 to 1/2 teaspoon yeast (dry or cake) in 1/3 cup warm water (warm!—not hot) and add 3/4 cup whole wheat flour. Stir a few times, cover, and leave it in a warm place for a few hours. This mixture will expand a bit, so be sure to use a container that is big enough. After a few hours the starter should be bubbly and light and fluffy. It will not be sour right away, but given a while longer it will be. This starter can now be stored in a clean, covered jar or crock in the refrigerator. This portion of starter that is saved before each new batch of bread is mixed and is stored in the refrigerator will be referred to as the primary starter.

The primary starter is now ready to be used. At least ten hours before mixing the bread dough together, more sourdough starter must be prepared. Empty the contents of the starter pot into a 4-quart mixing bowl and add 4 cups of whole wheat flour and 2 1/2 cups of warm water. Stir, but don't worry if all the lumps don't dissolve. They will take care of themselves during the fermentation process. Cover the bowl and let it stand in a warm place until it is ready to use.

The length of time the starter should be allowed to ferment depends upon two things—the temperature of the spot in which it is placed and the degree of sourness desired. The warmer the spot in which the starter is left, the more quickly it will ferment. The longer it is allowed to ferment, the sourer it will be. One quickly learns to tell when the starter is ready from its smell and appearance—it smells pungent, increases in volume, and bubbles. As a general rule, the starter should ferment for at least ten hours.

The sourness of the bread is also determined by two factors. The longer the starter is permitted to ferment, the sourer the bread. For very sour bread the starter should be allowed to ferment for 24-36 hours. The sourness of the primary starter from the pot will also affect that of the bread. The longer it has not been used, the sourer the bread will be. In determining how much time must be allowed for the starter to ferment, it is necessary to take both factors into consideration. One must experiment with different fermentation times to determine his sourness preference level. If the primary starter has been allowed to become too sour, it may be freshened before being used again. To freshen, add one tablespoon of the primary sour starter to 1/3 cup warm water and 3/4 cup of whole wheat flour. It is now ready to use.

There is one basic and very important rule which must be followed if the starter is to last and to provide good bread products. Before any other ingredient is added to it, about one cup of starter must be removed and put back into the clean pot or jar, covered, and refrigerated. This is the primary starter. Yeast should not be added again. Flour and water are all the starter needs to be freshened, and they provide all the nutrients necessary for yeast growth and reproduction. Forgetting to take out a cup of primary starter before adding other ingredients means buying another package of yeast or begging a little more starter from a sourdough friend.

The primary starter should be stored in the refrigerator rather than at room temperature. Unless the primary starter is used every day, storing it at room temperature invites the growth of undesirable bacteria and molds. Storing at cold temperatures is important because the starter is not a sterile yeast culture. The presence of other yeast, bacteria, and molds is not bad, but their growth should not be encouraged. Storage at a cold temperature does not harm the yeast, although it does reduce the reproduction rate considerably—to almost nothing compared to what happens at 80° F. When the primary starter is returned to a warm environment, the yeast become active again.

Remember from the earlier section on yeast fermentation that yeast breaks starches down into alcohol and carbon dioxide. The bubbles in the sponge are indications that carbon dioxide gas is escaping. Smell the sponge. That's the same alcohol that rises to the top of the starter pot and sometimes turns a dark color, depending upon the kind of flour or medium used. Many people think this liquid means the starter has spoiled. Not so; the starter is still good. Stir the alcohol into the rest of the starter, and it is ready to use.

PREPARATION
OF THE SOURDOUGH SPONGE

The sourdough sponge is the unbaked bread dough containing the starter, sweetening, salt, flavorings, and flour. Its preparation differs slightly from yeast sponges, but is basic and common to almost all sourdough bread recipes. The basic steps in the preparation of the sourdough sponge are described below.

1. The starter is stirred with the sweetening, salt, and flavorings in a large mixing bowl. The yeast is already active and in suspension in the starter.

2. The flour is added a little at a time and stirred in until the dough or sponge pulls away from the side of the bowl. Flour quantities, especially in sourdough recipes, can only be approximate because of differences in liquid absorption, compactness, and the amount of liquid present. The variation in liquid is peculiar to sourdough since the yeast breaks the flour starch down into alcohol and carbon dioxide gas during fermentation. Although this occurs in all yeast breads, the long and variable fermentation period of sourdough starter produces substantially more liquid alcohol.

3. The dough is turned out on a floured board and kneaded until it feels smooth and elastic. It should no longer be sticky and should spring back when pressed with the finger.

4. As with yeast breads, the dough may be given one or two risings. Two risings give a somewhat finer loaf, but one rising produces a highly satisfactory one, especially when it is well kneaded. If one rising is preferred, skip to Step 6. Although the directions for all the sourdough recipes specify one rising, they may be risen twice. To rise the sponge twice, shape the dough into a ball and place it in a greased bowl. Roll the dough in the bowl to coat its entire surface with oil. Cover it with a clean dish cloth and place it in a warm place to rise until it doubles in bulk. Sourdough sponges usually take 1 1/2-2 times longer to rise than yeast breads.

5. Punch the dough down and turn it out on a lightly floured board. Knead gently.

6. If a double recipe or a recipe for two loaves is used, divide the

dough into two equal parts. Shape the dough and place it in a greased loaf pan.

7. The dough may be brushed with a glaze at this point or just before it is placed in the oven. Brushing at this point is preferred because the glaze tends to keep the crust from drying out during the rising process.

8. Cover the dough with a clean dish cloth and set it in a warm place to rise. Allow the dough to rise until about double in bulk or until the top of the dough reaches about 1/2" to 3/4" above the rim of the pan. The bread will rise slightly more when baked.

9. Preheat the oven.

10. Bake until done.

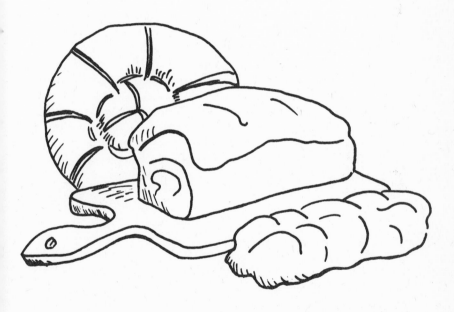

CONVERTING SOURDOUGH AND YEAST RECIPES

Any yeast recipe can be converted to sourdough. Whether it tastes good, however, is a different matter since the sour taste may conflict with another prominent flavor. For the most part, though, yeast recipes can be successfully converted to sourdough. Change in the other direction—from sourdough to yeast—is surer to produce less flavor conflict. The Sourdough may argue, of course, that the bread is blander and lacks the excitement, life, and aroma that only sourdough breads can emit. The choice is a matter of individual preference.

Converting a Yeast Recipe to Sourdough

There are only a few simple rules to convert yeast bread recipes to sourdough. For one large loaf of sourdough bread:
1. Omit the yeast.
2. Omit 1 3/4 cups liquids (liquids include not only water, milk, and juices, but eggs, which account for about 1/4 cup per large egg).
3. Add 2 cups sourdough starter.
4. Reduce the amount of flour by about 1 cup.

The ingredients are then mixed together by the basic method of preparing sourdough sponge.

To convert a recipe for two loaves of bread, double the directions—omit 3 1/2 cups of liquids, add 4 cups of starter, and reduce the amount of flour by about 2 cups.

In recipes where the essence of the bread comes from a liquid ingredient such as a pureé or eggs, lowering the fluid content by reducing the amounts of these ingredients may drastically alter its original flavor. In these instances, eliminate the milk or water, then reduce the amount of starter used. Oils should not be removed from the recipe. For an omission of every 1/4 cup of liquid, reduce the amount of starter used by 1/4 cup plus 1 1/2 teaspoons. As an example, to convert "Rich Egg Bread" (chapter 3) to sourdough:
1. Omit the yeast
2. Omit the 1 cup water
3. Add 1 1/4 cup minus 1 1/2 tablespoons sourdough starter
4. Reduce the amount of flour by about 1 cup

The rising time will be increased somewhat when the amount of starter is decreased.

Converting a Sourdough Recipe to Yeast

The reverse process is used in this case. For one large loaf of yeast bread:
1. Omit the sourdough starter
2. Add 1 1/2 teaspoon dry yeast
3. Add 1 3/4 cup warm liquid—milk or water
4. Increase the amount of flour by about 1 cup

The ingredients are then mixed together by the basic method of preparing the yeast bread sponge.

SOURDOUGH STARTER
(one recipe or 4-4 1/2 cups)

1 c. primary sourdough starter
from starter pot

2 1/2 c. warm water
4 c. whole wheat flour

Stir the starter, water, and flour together in a 4-quart bowl. The batter may be somewhat lumpy, but the lumps will disappear during the fermentation process. Cover the bowl with a plate or plastic wrap and let it sit in a warm place for 10-48 hours. The longer the starter sits and ferments, the sourer it becomes.

When the starter is ready to be used, stir thoroughly. Some alcohol may have risen to the top, and that should be blended into the starter.

Before this starter is used in any recipe, remove 1 cup and return it to the clean starter jar or crock and store it in the refrigerator. The remaining starter constitutes 1 recipe of sourdough starter.

BASIC WHOLE WHEAT SOURDOUGH BREAD
(two long loaves)

1 recipe sourdough starter	1 c. milk
3 T. honey	6 1/2 - 7 1/2 c. whole wheat
2 t. salt	flour

Prepare the sourdough starter the night before or at least 10 hours in advance.

In a large bowl, stir the starter, honey, salt, and milk. Slowly stir in the flour until the dough stiffens and pulls away from the side of the bowl.

Turn the dough out on a floured board and knead until it feels smooth and elastic. The dough should be fairly stiff.

Divide the dough into two equal parts. Shape into balls, and gently roll them out into cylinders about 3″ in diameter.

Sprinkle cornmeal on a cookie sheet.

Place the two long loaves on the cookie sheet. Brush with cream or liquid oil and cover with a clean dish cloth. Set in a warm place and allow to rise until about double in bulk.

Preheat the oven to 375° F.

Bake for 40 minutes or until done.

SOURDOUGH RYE BREAD
(two large loaves)

1 recipe sourdough starter	1 c. water
1/4 c. molasses	3 T. caraway seeds
2 t. salt	6 1/2 - 7 1/2 c. whole rye
2 T. liquid oil	flour
3 T. milk powder	

Prepare the sourdough starter the night before or at least 10 hours in advance.

Grease two large bread pans (9″ x 5″ x 2 3/4″).

In a large mixing bowl, stir together the starter, molasses, salt, oil, milk powder, water, and seeds. Slowly stir in the flour until the dough stiffens and pulls away from the side of the bowl.

Turn the dough out on a floured board and knead until it feels smooth and elastic and no longer sticks to the fingers.

Divide the dough into two equal parts, shape, and place in the greased pans. Cover with a clean dish cloth and set in a warm place to rise until about double in bulk.

Preheat the oven to 350° F.

Bake for 50-60 minutes or until done.

SOURDOUGH HERB BREAD
(two medium loaves)

1 recipe sourdough starter
1/4 c. raw sugar
1 T. salt
1/2 t. ginger, powdered

1/4 c. fresh parsley,
    finely minced
1/4 c. fresh basil,
    finely minced
4-6 c. whole wheat flour

Prepare the sourdough starter the night before or at least 10 hours in advance.

Grease two medium bread pans (8″ x 4″ x 2 3/4″).

In a large bowl, stir the starter, sugar, salt, ginger, parsley, and basil. Slowly add the flour until the dough pulls away from the side of the bowl.

Turn the dough out on a floured board and knead until it feels smooth and elastic.

Divide the dough into two equal parts, shape, and place in the greased pans. Cover with a clean dish cloth and set in a warm place to double in bulk.

Preheat the oven to 350° F.

Bake for 40-45 minutes or until done.

(*Note:* Any herb or combination of herbs may be used.)

SOURDOUGH CARROT BREAD
(two large loaves)

1 recipe sourdough starter	1 c. cooked carrot pureé
1 1/2 T. raw sugar	2 T. fresh parsley, minced
1 T. salt	6-7 c. whole wheat flour
1/2 c. milk	

Prepare the sourdough starter the night before or at least 10 hours in advance.

Grease two large bread pans (9″ x 5″ x 2 3/4″).

Prepare the carrot pureé. Cook two medium carrots in 1/4 cup water in a covered pot until soft. Place in a blender or food mill and pureé the carrots. Allow to cool.

In a large bowl, stir the starter, sugar, salt, milk, pureé, parsley, and 1 cup whole wheat flour. Slowly stir in the remaining flour until the dough starts to pull away from the side of the bowl.

Turn the dough out on a floured board and knead until it feels smooth and elastic, about 5-7 minutes.

Divide the dough into two equal parts, shape, and place in the greased pans. Brush the tops of the dough with milk, cover with a clean dish cloth and set in a warm place to double in bulk.

Preheat the oven to 350° F.

Bake for 50 minutes or until done.

HIGH PROTEIN SOURDOUGH BREAD
(two large loaves)

1 recipe sourdough starter	1 1/2 t. salt
2 T. honey	1 T. liquid oil
2/3 c. soy flour	1/2 c. water
1/2 c. skim milk powder	6-7 c. whole wheat flour

Prepare the starter the night before or at least 10 hours in advance.

Grease two large bread pans (9″ x 5″ x 2 3/4″).

In a large mixing bowl, stir the starter, honey, soy flour, milk powder, salt, oil, and water. Slowly stir in the wheat flour until the dough stiffens and pulls away from the side of the bowl.

Turn the dough out on a floured board and knead until it feels elastic and springs back at the touch, about 5-7 minutes.

Divide the dough into two equal parts, shape, and place in the greased pans. Cover with a clean dish cloth and set in a warm place to rise until about double in bulk.

Preheat the oven to 325° F.

Bake for 50-60 minutes or until done.

SOURDOUGH PUMPERNICKEL BREAD
(two large loaves)

1 recipe sourdough starter	2 T. liquid oil
1/4 c. cornmeal, plain	1 T. caraway seeds
3/4 c. water	1 c. mashed potatoes, cooled
1/4 c. molasses	4 c. whole rye flour
1 T. salt	2-3 c. whole wheat flour

Prepare the sourdough starter the night before or at least 10 hours in advance.

Grease two large bread pans (9″ x 5″ x 2 3/4″).

Combine the cornmeal and water in a saucepan and heat. Stir until the mixture thickens. Remove from the heat and allow this to cool before adding to the sponge.

In a large bowl, stir together the starter, molasses, salt, oil, seeds, cornmeal mixture, and mashed potatoes. Slowly stir in the rye flour, then the wheat flour until the dough pulls away from the side of the bowl.

Turn the dough out on a floured board and knead until it feels smooth and elastic.

Divide the dough into two equal parts, shape, and place in the greased pans. Brush with liquid oil, cover with a clean dish cloth, and set in a warm place. Allow the dough to rise until it is about 1/2" to 3/4" above the rim of the pan. Because this is such a heavy bread containing a relatively small proportion of whole wheat flour, rising may be a very slow process if the room temperature is less than 80-85°. To speed up rising, place the bread pans in a pan of very warm water—about 110° F. Add more warm water as needed to maintain the temperature.

Preheat the oven to 350° F.

Bake for 50-60 minutes or until done.

SOURDOUGH ONION RYE BREAD
(two large loaves)

1 recipe sourdough starter	3 T. caraway seeds
2 T. molasses	1 c. onion, minced finely
1 c. milk or water	2 c. whole wheat flour
1 T. salt	4 1/2 - 5 1/2 c. whole rye
1/4 c. liquid oil	flour

Prepare the sourdough starter the night before or at least 10 hours in advance.

Grease two large bread pans (9" x 5" x 2 3/4").

In a large bowl, stir the starter, molasses, milk, salt, oil, seeds, onion, and wheat flour. Slowly stir in the rye flour until the dough stiffens and pulls away from the side of the bowl.

Turn the dough out on a floured board and knead until it feels smooth and elastic, about 5-7 minutes.

Divide the dough into two equal parts, shape, and place in the greased pans. Brush the tops of the dough with liquid oil or cream, cover with a clean dish cloth, and set in a warm place to rise until about double in bulk.

Preheat the oven to 350° F.

Bake for 45-50 minutes or until done.

(Note: The proportion of wheat and rye flours may be varied according to one's personal taste. A high proportion of rye flour gives the bread a distinctively nutty flavor, although the loaves are relatively heavy.)

SOURDOUGH MOLASSES BREAD
(one large loaf)

2 c. sourdough starter	2 T. milk powder
1/4 c. molasses	2 T. liquid oil
1 t. salt	1/2 c. cornmeal, plain
2 T. soy flour	3-4 c. whole wheat flour

Prepare the starter the night before or at least 10 hours in advance.

Grease a large loaf pan (9″ x 5″ x 2 3/4″).

In a large mixing bowl, stir the starter, molasses, salt, soy flour, milk powder, oil, and cornmeal. Slowly add the flour until the dough pulls away from the side of the bowl.

Turn the dough out on a floured board and knead until it feels smooth and elastic and does not stick to the fingers.

Shape the dough and place in the greased pan. Brush with liquid oil, cover with a clean dish cloth, and place in a warm place until about double in bulk.

Preheat the oven to 350° F.

Bake for 50 minutes or until done.

SOURDOUGH RICE BREAD
(one large loaf)

2 c. sourdough starter	2 T. milk
2 T. raw sugar	1 c. rice flour
1/2 t. salt	2 1/2 - 3 c. whole wheat flour
1 T. liquid oil	

Prepare the sourdough starter the night before or at least 10 hours in advance.

Grease one large bread pan (9″ x 5″ x 2 3/4″).

In a large mixing bowl, stir the starter, sugar, salt, oil, milk, and rice flour. Slowly add the wheat flour until the dough pulls away from the side of the bowl.

Turn the dough out on a floured board and knead until it feels elastic and no longer sticks to the fingers.

Shape the dough and place it in the greased pan. Cover with a clean dish cloth and let sit in a warm place until about double in bulk.

Preheat the oven to 350° F.

Brush the top of the dough with cream or liquid oil.

Bake for 50 minutes or until done.

SOURDOUGH GARLIC BREAD
(one large loaf)

2 c. sourdough starter	2 T. milk
2 T. honey	2 T. butter, melted and cooled
1 t. salt	3-4 c. whole wheat flour
1/2 t. garlic powder	

Prepare the sourdough starter the night before or at least 10 hours in advance.

Grease one large bread pan (9″ x 5″ x 2 3/4″).

In a large mixing bowl, stir the starter, honey, garlic powder, milk, and butter. Slowly stir in the flour until the dough pulls away from the side of the bowl.

Turn the dough out on a floured board and knead until it feels smooth and elastic, about 5-7 minutes.

Shape the dough and place it in the greased pan. Cover with a clean dish cloth and set in a warm place to double in bulk.

Preheat the oven to 350° F.

Brush the top of the dough with cream or a beaten egg. Sprinkle sesame seeds over the top, if desired.

Bake for 45-50 minutes or until done.

SOURDOUGH BATTER BREAD
(one large loaf)

2 c. sourdough starter	2 T. soy flour
2 T. sugar	1/4 c. milk powder
1 t. salt	1/4 c. water
1 T. liquid oil	3-4 c. whole wheat flour

Prepare the sourdough starter the night before or at least 10 hours in advance.

Grease one large bread pan (9″ x 5″ x 3 3/4″).

In a large bowl, stir together the starter, sugar, salt, oil, soy flour, milk powder, and water. Slowly beat in the wheat flour until it becomes difficult to beat. Continue beating vigorously for 5 minutes.

Pour the batter into the greased pan. Cover with a clean dish cloth and set in a warm place to rise until the batter peeks over the rim of the pan.

Preheat the oven to 350° F.

Bake for 50 minutes or until done.

SOURDOUGH STEAMED BREAD
(one large loaf)

2 c. sourdough starter	1 T. liquid oil
2 T. raw sugar	3 - 3 1/2 c. whole wheat flour
1/2 t. salt	

Prepare the starter the night before or at least 10 hours in advance.

Grease one large bread pan (9" x 5" x 2 3/4").

In a large mixing bowl, stir together the starter, salt, sugar, and oil. Slowly add the flour until the dough begins to pull away from the side of the bowl.

Turn the dough out on a floured board and knead until it feels smooth and elastic. It should not be as stiff as dough for baking.

Shape the dough and place it in the greased pan.

Heat water in a steamer with a tight lid. The water should be almost as high as the steaming rack, but not touching the rack. Bring the water to a rolling boil.

Carefully place the bread pan on the steaming rack. The dough should not be allowed to double in bulk, although it may be allowed to rest for about 15 minutes prior to steaming.

Cover the pot and steam for about 40 minutes over water at a medium boil.

QUICK SOURDOUGH BREAD
(one large loaf)

1 t. dry yeast	3 T. milk powder
3 T. warm water	1 T. liquid oil
3 T. raw sugar	2 c. sourdough starter
1 t. salt	3 1/2 - 4 c. whole wheat flour

Prepare the sourdough starter the night before or at least 10 hours in advance.

Grease a large bread pan (9" x 5" x 2 3/4").

In a small bowl sprinkle the yeast over the water. Let stand until the yeast has dissolved, about 5 minutes.

In a large bowl, stir the sugar, salt, milk powder, oil, starter and yeast. Slowly add the whole wheat flour until the dough pulls away from the side of the bowl.

Turn the dough out on a floured board and knead until it feels elastic and no longer sticks to the fingers, about 5-7 minutes.

Shape the dough and place in the greased pan. Cover with a clean dish cloth and place in a warm place to rise until about double in bulk.

Preheat the oven to 350° F.

Bake for 50 minutes or until done.

SOURDOUGH ROLLS
(15-24 rolls)

2 c. sourdough starter	1 T. liquid oil
3 T. raw sugar	1 egg
1 t. salt	3 1/2 c. whole wheat flour
3 T. skim milk powder	

Prepare the starter the night before or at least 10 hours in advance.

Grease a cookie sheet or muffin tins, depending on the shape of rolls desired.

In a large mixing bowl, stir together the starter, sugar, salt, milk powder, oil, and egg. Slowly stir in the whole wheat flour until the dough pulls away from the side of the bowl.

Turn the dough out on a floured board and knead until it feels smooth and elastic. Shape into desired forms and place on a cookie sheet or in muffin tins to rise until double in bulk.

Preheat the oven to 350° F.

Brush the tops of the rolls with cream. Bake 15-25 minutes, depending on the size of the rolls, or until golden brown.

SOURDOUGH BISCUITS
(15-18 biscuits)

2 c. sourdough starter	2 T. liquid oil
1 T. raw sugar	2 t. baking powder
1/2 t. salt	1 1/2 c. whole wheat flour

Prepare the starter at least 10 hours in advance.

Lightly grease a cookie sheet.

In a medium-sized bowl, stir together the starter, sugar, salt, and oil. Add in the baking powder and flour and mix well.

Turn the dough out on a lightly floured board and knead gently. Roll the dough out to about 1/2" thick. Cut with a biscuit cutter or a drinking glass with a 2 1/2 - 3" diameter. Place the biscuits on the cookie sheet. Gently knead the scrap pieces of dough, roll out, and cut again.

Cover the biscuits with a clean dish cloth and let stand in a warm place for about 30 minutes.

Preheat the oven to 400° F.

Brush the tops of the biscuits with cream or an egg beaten with 1 T. water.

Bake for 20-25 minutes.

SOURDOUGH PANCAKES
(serves four)

1 recipe sourdough starter	1 egg, beaten
1/4 c. raw sugar	1/4 c. milk or cream
1/2 t. salt	1 1/2 t. baking soda
2 T. liquid oil	1/2 c. wheat germ

Prepare the starter the night before.

Heat a lightly greased griddle.

Beat together the starter, sugar, salt, oil, and egg. Stir in the milk, soda, and wheat germ.

Drop the batter by the tablespoonful onto the hot griddle to make small silver dollar-sized pancakes. Turn the pancakes when the bubbles begin to retain their holes.

SOURDOUGH BUCKWHEAT CAKES
(serves three to four)

1/2 c. sourdough starter	1 c. milk
1 1/2 c. buckwheat flour	2 T. liquid oil
1 c. water	1 egg, beaten
2 T. raw sugar	1 t. baking soda
1 t. salt	1/2 c. whole wheat flour

The night before preparing buckwheat cakes for breakfast, stir together the starter, buckwheat flour, and water in a large bowl, cover, and set aside in a warm place. Save some of the original starter since all of the buckwheat starter will be used.

Heat a lightly greased griddle.

To the buckwheat starter, add the sugar, salt, milk, oil, and egg. Beat vigorously. Slowly stir in the baking soda and flour. The batter will quickly start frothing and expanding.

Spoon out 2-3 inch cakes on the hot griddle. Turn the cakes when the bubbles begin to retain their holes.

BASIC SOURDOUGH CAKE

1/2 c. butter
3/4 c. raw sugar
2 eggs
1 c. milk
1 c. sourdough starter
2 t. baking powder

1/2 t. salt
1 T. grated lemon rind
1 t. vanilla or a
    favorite flavoring
2 1/2 c. whole wheat flour

Prepare the starter the night before or at least 10 hours in advance.

Preheat the oven to 350° F. Butter a 9-inch square pan and flour the bottom of the pan.

In a large mixing bowl, cream the butter and sugar. Add the eggs, beating in one at a time. Add the remaining ingredients in the order given, beating well after each addition.

Pour the batter into the baking pan. Shake the pan gently to level the batter.

Bake for 40 minutes or until the cake springs back when the center is gently touched with the finger.

SOURDOUGH CAROB CAKE

1/2 c. butter
3/4 c. raw sugar
2 eggs
1 c. milk
1 t. vanilla
1 t. cinnamon

3 1/2 T. carob powder,
    toasted
1/2 t. salt
1 c. sourdough starter
2 t. baking soda
2 c. whole wheat flour

Prepare the starter the night before or at least 10 hours in advance.

Preheat the oven to 325° F. Grease an 8-inch square baking pan and flour the bottom.

In a large mixing bowl, cream the butter and sugar. Beat in the eggs one at a time. Add the milk, vanilla, cinnamon, carob, salt, and starter. Beat vigorously for about 3-4 minutes by hand. Stir in the baking soda and flour and mix well.

Pour the batter into the greased pan and bake for 40-45 minutes or until done.

ROLLS
FOR EVERY MEAL

ROLLS ARE A perfect accompaniment to any meal and are as varied as the flaky, buttery croissant or the fruit-filled breakfast roll. They all may be prepared in advance, frozen, and reheated in foil.

ROLLS FROM YEAST
AND SOURDOUGH RECIPES

Any of the yeast and sourdough recipes may be used to make rolls. A recipe for a large loaf of bread will make between 12 and 24 rolls, depending on their size and shape.

To make rolls from yeast and sourdough bread recipes, prepare the dough as directed for bread. When the dough has been kneaded, form it into any of the shapes herein described. Like breads, it must be covered and allowed to rise until double in bulk. An egg, egg yolk, or cream glaze may be applied for a rich, golden brown crust, or butter may be brushed over the rolls when they are removed from the oven.

Baking times range from 15-25 minutes and vary with the size and the shape of the rolls. Rolls are usually baked at 350-375° F. and are done when they have reached a golden brown color. To store, allow them to cool throughly on a wire rack, wrap well in foil or plastic, and freeze. To prepare for serving, reheat in a moderate oven (350° F.) in tightly wrapped foil or in a moist paper bag until the rolls are hot. If reheating in a paper bag, use only plain brown ones— never use plastic-coated or shiny colored bags. To moisten the bag, partially fill it with water, shake it, then drain out the water. A dry bag may also be used, but moistening it helps to keep the rolls from drying out.

SHAPING ROLLS

The possibilities for roll shapes are limitless. The dough can be rolled out, cut, twisted, knotted, braided, folded, baked in forms, in pans, or on baking sheets. Some of the more conventional shapes are described below.

Basic Pan Rolls

Shape the dough into balls about 1 1/2 - 2 inches in diameter. Place them in greased cake pans about 1/2 inch apart.

Cloverleafs

Shape the dough into balls 3/4 to 1 inch in diameter and brush them with butter. Place three together in greased muffin cups.

Parker House

Roll the dough out to about 1/4 inch thick. Cut 2 1/2 - 3 inch circles with a biscuit cutter or a drinking glass. Brush with melted butter. Fold the dough over to form a half circle. Place on a greased baking sheet.

Butterhorns

Roll the dough out into a 10-12 inch circle about 1/4 inch thick. Brush with melted butter. With a thin and sharp knife, cut the circle into 16 equal parts. Roll each wedge beginning at the base and ending at the point. Place on a greased baking sheet.

Crescents

Prepare Butterhorns, then curve the ends inward to form crescents.

Swirls

Roll the dough 1/4 inch thick into a rectangle about 10 inches wide. Brush generously with melted butter. Sprinkle herbs, nuts, cinnamon, or fruit over it. Roll the dough like a jelly roll along its length. Cut into 1-inch slices and place cut-side down in greased muffin cups.

Butter Wrap-arounds

Roll the dough out into a rectangle 1/8 inch thick and about 6 inches wide. Brush generously with butter. Roll the dough along its length like a jelly roll. Slice into 2 1/2 to 3-inch sections and place on a greased baking sheet.

Crowns

Roll the dough out about 1/2 inch thick. Cut into pieces about 3 1/2 to 4 inches square. Bring each corner of the square to the center and press. Place on a greased baking sheet.

Bread Sticks

There are two ways of making bread sticks.

1) Roll the dough out about 1/2 inch thick. With a very sharp knife, cut into strips about 1/2 inch thick. Gently roll each strip with the hands to round the edges. Cut into desired lengths.

2) Form balls of dough about 1 1/2 - 2 inches in diameter. Roll each ball with the hands to form a rope about 1/2 inch in diameter. Cut into desired lengths. Place on greased baking sheets.

Snails

Form ropes of dough by rolling long bread sticks. Place one end of the rope on a greased baking sheet and coil the rope around it to resemble a snail's shell. When the desired size is reached, cut the rope of dough. Tuck the end of the coil under.

Braids

Form ropes of dough by rolling long bread sticks. Place 3 ropes of dough side by side and braid them. Cut the braids into 3 1/2 - 4 inch sections. Pinch the ends of each section and place on greased baking sheets.

Knots

Form ropes of dough by rolling long bread sticks. Knot the dough using one or two ropes at a time to create a variety of knots.

LARGE BREAKFAST OR "COFFEE" ROLLS

Bread dough, particularly sweet dough, may be rolled out and filled with lightly sweetened fruit, jam, nuts, or any of the pastry fillings (see later this chapter) to make a large ring, braids, swirled rolls, crescents, and other shapes. One large roll serves 6-12 persons. Although the rolls can look beautiful and intricate, they are usually very simple to make.

After the rolls are shaped, they should be glazed with an egg glaze and may be sprinkled with poppy or sesame seeds, chopped fruit, or nuts. Allow the rolls to rise until about double in bulk. Bake in a moderate oven (350° F.) about 35 minutes or until done.

Swirled Rolls

These are made like jelly rolls. Roll the dough out into a rectangle about 1/4 inch thick and 12 inches wide. Spread a pastry filling over it or generously brush with melted butter and sprinkle with nuts. Roll the dough along its length like a jelly roll. Place on a greased baking sheet with the seam-side down. The roll may be curved or twisted or shaped into a circle.

Rings

A large variety of rings are possible. Some are filled while others have fruit, nuts, and spices added to the dough. Some are rolled like jelly rolls, others are braided and twisted. A few are described below, but different fillings and shapes may also be combined.

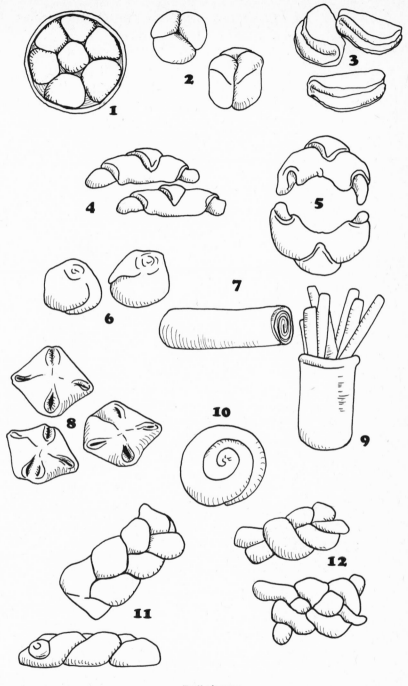

Roll shapes

1 - Basic pan rolls   2 - Cloverleafs   3 - Parker House
4 - Butterhorns   5 - Crescents   6 - Swirls   7 - Butter Wrap-arounds
8 - Crowns   9 - Bread sticks   10 - Snails   11 - Braids   12 - Knots

Scandinavian Rings

Roll the dough out 1/4 inch thick into rectangles about 12″ x 15″. Sprinkle about 1 1/2 cups of chopped dried fruit and nuts over it. Roll the dough along its length like a jelly roll into a long cylinder. Shape the roll into a ring, seam-side down on a greased baking sheet. Carefully pinch the ends together to complete the ring. The ring may now be cut in one of two ways:

1) With a knife or scissors, cut through about 3/4 of the outside edge of the ring leaving the center portion intact. Make cuts every 1 1/2 inches. Turn each piece to lay on one of the cut sides so that the spirals show.

2) With a knife or scissors; cut through the *top* 3/4 of the ring leaving the bottom portion intact. Make cuts every 1 inch. Turn every other piece on its side to the outside. Turn the remaining alternate pieces on their sides towards the inside of the ring.

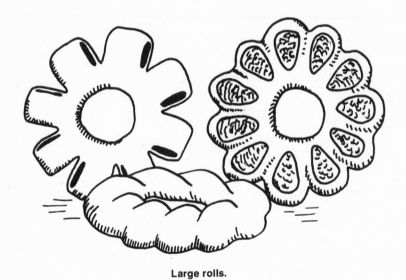

Large rolls.

Fruit Rings

Roll the dough out into a 1/4 inch thick rectangle 8″ x 18″. Spread sweetened fruit or jam in the center down the length of the dough. Roll the sides of the dough over the filling, pinching the seam to seal it. Turn the roll over, seam side down and form a circle on a greased baking sheet. Pinch the ends together to complete the circle. Make cuts in the ring to the filling about 1 1/2 inches apart and extending from about 1/2 inch from the outer edge of the ring to 1/2 inch from the inner edge. As the dough rises, the cuts will open to expose the fruit filling.

Braided Rings

Add 1/2 cup chopped nuts, 3/4 cup raisins or chopped dates, 1 teaspoon cinnamon, and 1/4 teaspoon nutmeg to the dough. Divide the dough into three equal parts and make 3 ropes of dough, about 1 inch in diameter. Place the ropes side by side on a greased baking sheet and braid. Shape into a circle, and pinch the ends together to complete the ring.

Crescents

They are made like rings, only the ends are not joined to form a circle, rather they are open and resemble a quarter moon.

Filled Braids

Roll the dough out into a rectangle about 3/8 inch thick and about 10 inches wide. Place on a greased baking sheet. Place pastry filling in the middle down the length of the dough. With a sharp knife, cut the dough on either side of the filling into 1-inch strips. The cuts may be made perpendicular to the filling or slightly diagonal. Fold the strips over alternately to braid. Pinch the ends to seal in the filling.

DINNER ROLLS
(2 - 3 1/2 dozen)

1 T. dry yeast	2 T. butter
1 1/2 c. warm water	1 egg
3 T. raw sugar	3-4 c. whole wheat flour
1 t. salt	

Grease cookie sheets or muffin tins, depending on the shapes of rolls desired.

In a large bowl, sprinkle the yeast over the water. Allow the yeast to dissolve, about 5 minutes. Stir in the sugar, salt, butter, and egg. Slowly stir in the flour until the dough pulls away from the side of the bowl.

Turn the dough out on a floured board and knead until it feels elastic, about 5-7 minutes.

Shape the dough into rolls. Their size determines the number baked. Place on greased baking pans. Cover with a clean dish cloth and set in a warm place to rise until about double in bulk.

Preheat the oven to 350° F.

The rolls may be glazed with cream or beaten eggs before baking, or they may be brushed with butter as soon as they come out from the oven.

Bake for 15 minutes or until the rolls are a golden brown.

SEMMEL
(one dozen)

1 T. dry yeast	2 T. butter, melted
1 1/2 c. warm water	4 - 4 1/2 c. whole wheat flour
1/2 t. salt	

Grease a large baking sheet.

In a large bowl, sprinkle the yeast over the warm water. Allow the yeast to dissolve, about 5 minutes. Stir in the salt and butter. Slowly add the flour until the dough pulls away from the side of the bowl.

Turn the dough out on a floured board and knead until smooth and elastic.

Divide the dough into about 12 equal parts. Shape each part into a ball. Flatten the balls until about 1 inch thick; the finished rolls will be about 3". Using a thin and very sharp knife, make curved cuts in the top of the dough beginning about 1/16 inch from the center and curving to the side. (See illustration.) Make 5 cuts around the roll, but do not allow any of the cuts to intersect in the middle.

Semmels.

Place the rolls on the greased baking sheet. Cover with a clean dish cloth and place in a warm place to rise until about double in bulk.

Preheat the oven to 350° F.

Brush the tops of the semmels with liquid oil or melted butter.

Bake for 25-30 minutes or until done.

BRIOCHE
(for about 16)

1 T. dry yeast	1/2 c. milk
1/4 c. warm water	1 egg, separated
1/2 c. butter	4 eggs, beaten
1/4 c. raw sugar	3 1/2 - 4 c. whole wheat flour
1/4 t. salt	

In a small bowl or cup, sprinkle the yeast over the warm water. Allow to dissolve.

Cream the butter and sugar. Stir in the salt, egg yolk, and the eggs, beating them in one at a time. Stir in the milk and yeast. Add the flour and stir to make a soft dough.

Cover and allow to rise until double in bulk.

Stir the dough down, cover the bowl with foil or a plastic wrap and refrigerate overnight or for several hours.

Butter brioche forms or muffin tins.

Stir the dough down and turn out on a lightly floured board, but do not knead. Cut off about 1/5 of the dough and reserve. Divide the remaining dough into 16 equal parts and shape into balls. Flatten the balls slightly and place in the brioche forms or muffin tins.

Divide the reserved dough into 16 equal parts. Shape each part into an egg-shaped ball. With a finger, make an indentation in the center of each brioche. Place the pointed end of the ball into the indentation.

Cover with a clean dish cloth and place in a warm place to rise until about double in bulk or until the top ball is above the rim of the form.

Preheat the oven to 425° F.

Prepare the egg wash by beating the egg white with 1 tablespoon water.

Brush the brioche with the egg wash.

Bake for 15 minutes or until golden brown.

CROISSANTS
(for about 3 dozen)

2 c. butter	1 t. salt
4 c. whole wheat flour	1 1/4 c. milk or water

In a large mixing bowl, stir together the flour, salt, and milk.

Turn the dough out on a lightly floured board and knead for at least 10 minutes. Successful puff pastry depends on its highly developed gluten to stretch into paper thin layers without tearing. Kneading is necessary to develop the gluten—and elasticity—in the dough.

Shape the dough into a ball. Wrap in a clean dish cloth or a plastic wrap if your refrigerator is a frost-free model. Chill for about 1 hour.

While the dough chills, shape the butter into a block about 4-5 inches square. Place the butter between two big sheets of waxed paper and roll it out into a square about 1/4 inch thick. Refrigerate.

When the dough has chilled and is ready to be rolled, check the consistency of the butter. If the butter has cooled too much and become very hard, remove it from the refrigerator and allow it to warm until an impression is left when it is lightly pressed with the finger.

Roll the chilled dough into a rectangle about 10″ x 24″.

Cut the butter in half to form two rectangles. Place one slab of butter in the center of the dough. Fold one side of the dough over it to cover it completely. Place the other slab of butter on top of it. Fold over the remaining leaf of dough. Seal the butter in by pinching the seams together.

Carefully roll the dough out without tearing it to form a rectangle about 9 x 20. Fold the ends in *to* the center line, then fold it *along* the center line to form 4 layers of dough.

Wrap the dough in a clean dish cloth or plastic wrap and refrigerate for 1 hour. Refrigeration between rolling out and folding the dough is part of the necessary temperature control. The dough must be cool enough to hold its shape, and warm enough to be rolled without tearing the thin layers of dough.

If the whole wheat flour used contains coarse particles of germ and bran, the dough should not be folded any further. There are 9 layers, each separated from the other by butter. Folding it further may cause the dough to tear because of the coarse particles. The dough is now ready to be rolled out into croissants.

If the flour is very finely ground with no coarse flakes of bran and germ, it may again be rolled out gently and folded. Once again roll out the dough into a rectangle about 9″ x 20″. Fold the ends to the center, then fold again along the center line. Wrap it in the dish cloth or plastic wrap and refrigerate for another hour. The dough is now ready to be rolled out into croissants.

Making Croissants.

Cut the dough in half. Re-wrap one half and return it to the refrigerator.

On a lightly floured board, roll the dough out into a rectangle about 1/8 inch thick. Using a thin and very sharp knife, cut the dough into strips about 5-6 inches wide. Cut the strips into triangles with bases of about 3 - 3 1/2 inches.

Beginning with the wide base, roll each triangle towards the point. Gently pull the ends as the dough is being rolled and try to maintain symmetry on both sides. Curve the ends of the rolls to form crescents. Place on an ungreased cookie sheet. The rolling must be done quickly before the dough softens and the butter melts.

Place the rolls in the refrigerator to chill.

Roll out the other half of the dough and repeat.

Chill the croissants for at least one hour.

Preheat the oven to 475° F.

Reshape the rolls, if necessary, curving the ends to form crescents.

Brush with a glaze made with 1 egg beaten with 1 T. water.

Bake at 475° F. for 5 minutes, then lower the temperature to 350° F. and bake an additional 8-10 minutes or until a light golden brown.

RICH BREAKFAST ROLLS
(makes 18-20)

2 T. dry yeast	1/2 c. butter or lard, melted
1/2 c. warm water	1/2 t. salt
3/4 c. milk	2 eggs
1/2 c. sugar	4 1/2 - 5 c. whole wheat flour

Grease cookie sheets, muffin tins, or cake pans, depending on the shapes of rolls desired.

In a large bowl, sprinkle the yeast over the warm water. Allow the yeast to dissolve, about 5 minutes. Stir in the milk, sugar, butter, salt, and eggs. Slowly add the flour until the dough pulls away from the side of the bowl.

Turn the dough out on a floured board and knead until it feels elastic, about 5-7 minutes.

Shape the dough into rolls (their size determines the number made) and place them on the greased baking pans. Cover with a clean dish cloth and set in a warm place to rise until about double in bulk.

Preheat the oven to 350° F.

Brush the tops with cream or an egg glaze. Sprinkle with poppy or sesame seeds, if desired.

Bake for 15-20 minutes or until done.

BASIC SWEET ROLL DOUGH
(for about 24-36 rolls)

2 T. dry yeast	2 eggs, lightly beaten
1/2 c. warm water	3/4 c. warm milk
2 T. butter, melted	1 t. grated lemon rind
3/4 c. raw sugar	4 1/2 c. whole wheat flour
1/2 t. salt	

In a large mixing bowl, sprinkle the yeast over the water. Allow the yeast to dissolve, about 5 minutes. Add the butter, sugar, salt, eggs, milk, and grated lemon rind. Stir well. Slowly stir in the flour until the dough pulls away from the sides of the bowl.

Turn the dough out on a floured board and knead for 5-7 minutes or until it feels smooth and elastic. This dough should not be as stiff as bread dough.

Roll the dough out, cut into desired shapes, and fill with a favorite filling. Any of the shapes and fillings for Danish pastry may be used.

Brush with an egg glaze. Allow to rise until about double in bulk.

Bake at 350° F. until golden brown.

DANISH PASTRY
(two dozen)

1 T. dry yeast
3 T. raw sugar
1 1/4 c. milk, warm
1 egg, beaten
4 1/2 - 5 c. whole wheat flour
1 1/2 c. butter, sweet

Egg Glaze:
1 egg, beaten
1 T. water or milk

In a large mixing bowl, sprinkle the yeast over the warm milk. Allow the yeast to dissolve, about 5-10 minutes.

While the yeast dissolves, shape the butter into a block about 4-5 inches square. Flour may be sprinkled over it to facilitate handling. Place the butter between two large sheets of waxed paper and roll it out into a square about 1/4 inch thick. Refrigerate if the butter is very soft.

Stir the egg into the yeast and add the flour to form a fairly soft dough.

Turn the dough out onto a well floured board and sprinkle flour over the dough to ease handling. Knead until the dough is smooth, about 5 minutes.

Roll the dough out into a rectangle about 10" x 20".

Cut the square slab of butter in half and place it in the center of the dough. Fold over one side of the dough. Place the other slab of butter over the layered dough, and cover it with the other leaf of dough. Seal the butter in completely by pinching the seams together.

Roll the dough out into a rectangle of the same size (about 10" x 20"). Fold into three layers in the same way as before.

Roll and fold the dough once more. If the butter begins to melt and squeeze out, refrigerate the dough for about 30 minutes.

The dough is now ready to be used for making pastries. It may be cut into thirds and made into different shapes. Refrigerate dough that is not being used.

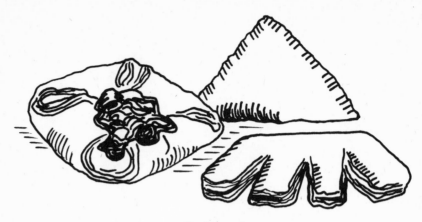

Danish pastry.

PASTRY SHAPES

Three basic shapes of Danish pastry are triangles, cockscombs, and circles. Each is detailed next.

Triangles

Roll the pastry dough out to about 1/4 inch thick. With a thin and very sharp knife, cut the dough into squares about 3" x 3". Place 1 tablespoon of jam, jelly, or pastry filling in the center. Fold the dough over to form a triangle, encasing the filling. Seal by pressing a fork over the edges. Brush with the egg glaze. Refrigerate until it is baked.

Cockscombs

Roll the pastry dough out to about 1/4 inch thick. With a thin and very sharp knife, cut the dough into strips about 4 - 4 1/2" wide. Place pastry filling in the center down the length of the strips. Fold the dough over the filling. Gently press the edges together. Make cuts about 1/2" deep and about 3/4" apart on the edge of the rolled dough. Cut into sections about 2 1/2 - 3" long. Brush with the egg glaze. Refrigerate until baked.

Circles

Roll the dough out to about 1/4 inch thick. With a thin and very sharp knife, cut the dough into squares about 3" x 3". Bring each corner in to the center and gently press. Brush with the egg glaze. Drop a tablespoon of filling or jam or jelly into the indentation at the center. Refrigerate until baked.

Preheat the oven to 400° F.

Place the pastries on ungreased cookie sheets leaving ample space between them.

Bake for 15-20 minutes or until lightly browned.

FILLINGS —
LEMON CREAM FILLING
(eight pastries)

1/2 c. milk	1 egg, well beaten
1 T. whole wheat flour	3 T. lemon juice
1/4 c. raw sugar	1 t. grated lemon rind

Add all of the ingredients to a small saucepan.

Cook, stirring constantly, over low heat until the filling is thick.

Cool the filling thoroughly before using.

APPLESAUCE FILLING
(eight pastries)

1/2 c. applesauce,	1 T. whole wheat flour
thick and unsweetened	3 T. honey
1 t. lemon juice	

Stir all of the ingredients in a small saucepan.

Cook, stirring constantly, over low heat until the filling thickens.

Cool the filling thoroughly.

VANILLA CREAM FILLING
(eight pastries)

1/2 c. milk
1 T. whole wheat flour   2 T. raw sugar
1 egg, well beaten   1 t. vanilla extract

Stir together all the ingredients except the vanilla in a small saucepan.

Heat and cook over a low flame, stirring constantly, until the filling thickens.

Remove from the heat, stir in the vanilla, and allow the filling to cool thoroughly.

PINEAPPLE FILLING
(eight pastries)

1/2 c. crushed pineapple   2 T. honey
    unsweetened   1 T. whole wheat flour

Stir together all the ingredients in a small saucepan.

Heat and cook over a low flame, stirring constantly, until the filling thickens.

Allow to cool thoroughly.

NUT FILLING
(eight pastries)

1/2 c. nuts, chopped   1/4 c. raw sugar
1/3 c. milk   1 T. whole wheat flour

Stir together the milk, sugar, and flour in a small saucepan.

Cook over low heat, stirring constantly, until thick.

Stir in the chopped nuts and allow to cool thoroughly.

DRIED FRUIT FILLING
(eight pastries)

2/3 c. dried fruit,
  chopped fine

3 T. honey

Stir the fruit and honey together.

CINNAMON ROLLS
(18-20 rolls)

1 recipe "Dinner Rolls"
1/4 c. butter, melted

1/2 c. raw sugar
1 T. cinnamon

Grease two round cake pans.

In a small bowl, stir together the sugar and cinnamon.

Prepare the dough for 1 recipe Dinner Rolls.

Roll the dough out into a rectangle about 9″ x 18″. Brush the dough with the melted butter. Sprinkle the cinnamon-sugar over the butter.

Roll the dough jelly-roll fashion into a cylinder about 18 inches long.

Cut the roll into 1-inch slices. Place the slices, cut side down fairly close to each other in the cake pans.

Cover with a clean dish cloth and allow to rise until about double in bulk.

Preheat the oven to 350° F.

Bake for 25 minutes or until brown.

PECAN CROWNS
(12 rolls)

1 recipe "Rich
  Breakfast Rolls"
1/4 c. butter, melted
1/3 c. raw sugar
1 t. cinnamon

Topping:
1/2 c. raw sugar
2 T. maple syrup
1/3 c. butter
1/2 c. pecans, chopped

Grease 12 muffin cups.

Prepare the topping by heating the sugar, syrup, and butter in a saucepan until the sugar crystals dissolve.

Place the chopped pecans in the bottoms of the muffin cups. Pour the butter-sugar topping over the pecans.

Prepare the dough for Rich Breakfast Rolls.

Roll the dough out into a rectangle about 8″ x 18″. Brush with 1/4 c. melted butter. Sprinkle the sugar and cinnamon evenly over it. Roll the dough in jelly-roll fashion to form an 18-inch cylinder.

Cut the roll of dough into 1 1/2″ slices. Place each slice in the muffin cups over the topping.

Cover with a clean dish cloth and allow to rise until about double in bulk.

Preheat the oven to 350° F.

Bake for 25 minutes or until done. Remove the rolls from the muffin tins immediately after taking them out from the oven. Cool and serve the rolls upside down so that the pecans are at the top.

KOLACHES
(about 24)

2 T. dry yeast	4 egg yolks
1 c. warm milk	4 - 4 1/2 c. whole wheat flour
2/3 c. butter	1 1/2 c. tart plum or
1/3 c. raw sugar	apricot jam
1/2 t. salt	

Grease two large cookie sheets.

In a large bowl, sprinkle the yeast over the warm milk and allow it to dissolve, about 5 minutes. Add the butter and stir until it dissolves. Stir in the sugar, salt, and egg yolks. Stir in the flour until the dough pulls away from the bowl.

Without kneading, divide the dough into about 24 equal parts. Roll each piece into a ball and place about 3″ apart on the cookie sheets. Greased hands may make the dough easier to handle.

With a finger, make an indentation large enough for 1 tablespoon of filling in the center of each ball. Place 1 tablespoon tart plum or apricot jam in each indentation.

Cover with a clean dish cloth and place in a warm place to rise until double in bulk.

Preheat the oven to 350° F.

Bake 15-20 minutes or until lightly browned.

JAPANESE MANJU
(15 manjus)

1 1/2 T. butter	Bean Filling (optional):
3/4 c. raw sugar	1/4 c. dried beans
2 eggs	(kidney, lima,
1/4 c. milk	pinto, navy, etc.)
1/4 t. salt	1/4 c. raw sugar
1 T. baking powder	
2 1/2 c. whole wheat flour	

Prepare the beans in advance. Cook the beans in water until soft. Drain, then place in a blender to puree. Stir in the sugar and allow the filling to cool.

Grease one large baking sheet.

Stir together the butter and sugar. Beat in the eggs. Stir in the remaining ingredients.

Place the dough in the refrigerator to chill for about 30 minutes to make the dough easier to handle.

Preheat the oven to 350° F.

Divide the dough into about 15 equal parts. Shape each part into a ball. Flatten the ball until about 1/4 inch thick. Place one teaspoon of cooled bean filling in the center of the dough. Bring the edges of the dough together to seal in the filling.

Place the manju, seam-side down, on the greased baking sheet.

Prepare an egg glaze by beating 1 egg with 1 tablespoon milk or cream. Brush the glaze over the tops of the manju. Sprinkle sesame or poppy seeds over the glaze.

Bake for 20 minutes or until done.

CINNAMON-PECAN BRAIDS
(two long braids)

2 T. dry yeast	1 T. cinnamon, powdered
1/2 c. warm water	1/2 c. pecans, chopped
2/3 c. sugar	3/4 c. raisins
1 1/2 c. milk	6 - 6 1/2 c. whole wheat flour
1 t. salt	pecan halves
1/4 c. liquid oil	

Lightly grease one cookie sheet.

In a large bowl, sprinkle the yeast over the water and allow it to dissolve, about 5 minutes. Add the sugar, milk, salt, oil, and cinnamon, and stir well. Slowly add the flour until the dough begins to pull away from the side of the bowl. Add the chopped pecans and raisins, and mix in.

Turn the dough out on a floured board and knead until the dough feels elastic, about 5 minutes.

Divide the dough into six equal parts and shape into balls. Roll each ball into ropes about 15 inches long.

Place three ropes of dough side by side on the greased cookie sheet and braid. Join the three ropes at the ends by bringing them together and pinching. Repeat for the remaining three ropes of dough.

Brush the tops with an egg glaze. Decorate with pecan halves.

Cover with a clean dish cloth and place in a warm spot to rise until double in bulk.

Preheat the oven to 350° F.

Bake for 25 minutes or until a golden brown.

APPLE RING
(two medium rings)

1 T. dry yeast
1 1/2 c. warm water
1/4 c. sugar
1/4 c. honey
1/4 c. milk powder
2 T. oil or melted butter
1 t. salt
2 eggs, beaten
6 - 6 1/2 c. whole wheat flour

Filling:
1 1/2 c. apple sauce
3 c. apples, sliced 1/4" thick
1/4 t. cinnamon
2 T. honey

Glaze:
1 egg, well beaten
   with 1 T. water
pecan halves

Lightly grease a large cookie sheet.

In a small bowl, prepare the filling by stirring the applesauce with the cinnamon and honey. Set aside.

In a large bowl, sprinkle the yeast over the water. Allow the yeast to dissolve, about 5 minutes. Stir in the sugar, honey, milk powder, oil, salt, and eggs. Slowly add the flour until the dough pulls away from the side of the bowl.

Turn the dough out on a floured board and knead until it feels smooth and elastic, about 5-7 minutes.

Divide the dough into two equal parts. Shape each part into a ball and roll into a rectangle about 8" x 14". Arrange half of the sliced apples down the length in the middle of the dough. Spoon half of the applesauce over the apples. Carefully lap the sides of the dough over the filling. Pinch the seam together to seal it. Gently lift the roll, turn it upside down and place it on the cookie sheet in a ring. Carefully pinch the two ends together to complete the ring. Make cuts in the ring about 1 1/2" apart.

Brush the top with the egg glaze. Place pecan halves between the cuts in the ring.

Allow to rise until about double in bulk.

Preheat the oven to 350° F.

Bake for 25 minutes or until golden brown.

NUT RING
(one large ring)

1 T. dry yeast	Nut Filling:
3/4 c. warm milk	1/4 c. butter, melted
3 T. raw sugar	1/4 c. raw sugar
1/2 t. salt	3/4 c. nuts, chopped
3 T. butter, melted	
1/4 t. cinnamon or mace	
1 egg	
3 - 3 1/2 c. whole wheat flour	

Grease a large cookie sheet.

In a large bowl, sprinkle the yeast over the milk and allow it to dissolve, about 5 minutes. Stir in the sugar, salt, butter, cinnamon, and egg. Slowly add the flour until the dough pulls away from the bowl.

Turn the dough out on a floured board and knead until it feels smooth and elastic, about 5-7 minutes.

Roll the dough out into a rectangle about 10" x 15". Brush with the melted butter. Sprinkle the sugar and nuts over it.

Roll the dough along its length like a jelly roll into a 15 inch cylinder. Seal the seams.

Place the roll on the cookie sheet in a ring, seam-side down. Gently pinch the ends together to seal the ring.

With a thin and very sharp knife, make cuts into the outside edge of the ring about 1 1/2 inches apart, leaving about 3/4 inch of the center portion of the ring intact. Turn each of the cut pieces on its side.

Cover with a clean dish cloth and allow to rise until about double in bulk.

Preheat the oven to 350° F.

Brush the top with cream or an egg glaze.

Bake for 25-30 minutes or until golden brown.

STOLLEN
(one large stollen)

2 T. dry yeast
1 c. warm milk
2/3 c. raw sugar
1/2 t. salt
2/3 c. butter, melted
2 eggs
1/2 t. cinnamon
1/4 t. nutmeg or mace
2 T. grated lemon rind
3 1/2 - 4 c. whole wheat flour

1/2 c. raisins
1/2 c. nuts, chopped
1/2 c. chopped cranberries
  or dried dates or figs

Glaze:
1 egg yolk
1 T. cream
pecan halves or whole almonds

Grease a large cookie sheet.

In a large bowl, sprinkle the yeast over the warm milk. Allow the yeast to dissolve, about 5 minutes. Stir in the sugar, salt, butter, eggs, cinnamon, nutmeg, and lemon rind. Slowly add in the flour and stir until the dough stiffens and pulls away from the side of the bowl. Stir in the raisins, nuts, and fruit.

Turn the dough out on a floured board and knead until it feels smooth and elastic, and no longer sticks to the fingers (about 5-7 minutes).

Shape the dough into a ball, then roll out into an oval about 8" x 12". Fold the dough over lengthwise with the top layer about 1/2 inch narrower than the bottom layer.

Beat the egg yolk with the cream and brush on the stollen. Decorate the top with pecan halves or whole almonds.

Cover with a clean dish cloth and set in a warm place to rise until about double in bulk.

Preheat the oven to 350° F.

Bake for 40-45 minutes or until done.

ONION-CARAWAY OVALS
(three large oval rolls)

1 recipe "Dinner Rolls"	1 egg
3/4 c. onions, chopped finely	3 t. caraway seeds
1/4 c. butter, melted	

In a small bowl, beat together the butter and egg. Set aside.

Prepare one recipe Dinner Rolls.

Divide the dough into 3 equal parts. Roll out into oval pieces about 1/4 inch thick. Brush the butter-egg mixture over the dough. Sprinkle 1/4 cup onions and one teaspoon caraway seeds over each oval piece. With the back of a tablespoon, press the onions gently onto the dough to ensure that they will adhere.

Place the rolls on a greased cookie sheet. Cover with a clean dish cloth and set in a warm place to rise until about double in bulk.

Preheat the oven to 325° F.

Bake for 25 minutes or until a light golden brown.

CHEESE CRACKERS
(about three dozen)

1 c. whole wheat flour	1/2 c. butter
1 c. grated cheddar cheese, mild	2 T. fresh parsley, chopped

Stir together the cheese and flour. Add in the butter and mix well until thoroughly blended. Stir in the chopped parsley.

Place the mixture in the refrigerator for about 30 minutes to cool. This will make the dough easier to handle.

Roll the dough out on a floured board until about 1/8 inch thick. Cut with a 2 - 2 1/4 inch drinking glass or cookie cutter. Place on an ungreased baking sheet about 1/2 inch apart.

Preheat the oven to 275° F.

Bake for 17 minutes or until the crackers barely begin to brown.

CHAPTER 6

MAKING
CRUMBLY QUICK BREADS

QUICK BREADS, UNLIKE yeast breads, rely on baking powder for leavening. Thus, they do not require kneading or proofing prior to baking. Quick breads can hardly be compared to yeast or sourdough breads because they are a very different product. Soft wheat or all-purpose flour is used since the development of gluten is neither required nor desired. Because their texture is crumbly, they are unsuitable for sandwiches. They tend to be sweeter—many are much more like a heavy cake—and are perfect for the morning or afternoon tea. Muffins, pancakes, and doughnuts are also included with quickbreads.

BANANA BREAD
(one large loaf)

1/4 c. butter	1/2 t. salt
1/4 c. honey	2 t. baking powder
1/4 c. raw sugar	2 c. whole wheat flour
2 eggs	1 T. grated lemon rind
1 c. bananas, mashed	1/2 c. nuts, chopped
(about 2 medium)	(optional)

Preheat the oven to 325° F. Butter a large loaf pan (9" x 5" x 2 3/4").

Cream together the butter, honey, and sugar. Add the eggs, beating in one at a time. Stir in the remaining ingredients and mix well.

Pour the batter into the buttered pan.

Bake for 50 minutes or until done.

DATE NUT BREAD
(one large loaf)

1/2 c. dates, pitted	1 T. grated lemon rind
and chopped	1/2 c. bran flakes
1 c. boiling water	1 t. baking powder
2 T. butter	1/2 t. salt
3/4 c. raw sugar	1 1/2 c. whole wheat flour
1 egg	1/2 c. nuts, chopped

Preheat the oven to 350° F. Grease a 9" x 5" x 2 3/4" loaf pan.

In a small mixing bowl, combine the water and dates and allow them to cool.

In a large mixing bowl, cream the butter and raw sugar until the sugar has dissolved. Add the egg and grated lemon rind and beat vigorously. Add the bran flakes, stir, then stir in the date mixture. Add the remaining ingredients and mix well.

Pour the batter into the greased pan. Bake for 50 minutes or until done.

CRANBERRY LOAF
(one large loaf)

2 T. butter
2 T. liquid oil
3 T. honey
1/2 c. raw sugar
1 egg
1/2 c. milk
1/2 c. orange juice
2 T. soy flour

2 t. baking powder
1 t. grated lemon rind
1 c. cranberries,
  chopped
2 c. whole rye flour
1/2 c. chopped nuts
  (optional)

Preheat the oven to 350° F. Grease a 9″ x 5″ x 2 3/4″ pan.

In a large mixing bowl, cream the butter, oil, honey, and sugar. Beat in the egg. Add the milk, soy flour, baking powder, and 1 cup of the rye flour, stirring after each addition. Stir in the orange juice, lemon rind, and the remaining rye flour. Mix in the cranberries and nuts.

Pour the batter into the greased loaf pan. Bake for 50 minutes or until done.

HONEY LOAF
(one large loaf)

2 T. butter
1 c. honey
1 egg
2 T. grated orange rind
3/4 c. orange juice

1 T. baking powder
1/2 t. salt
2 c. whole wheat flour
3/4 c. chopped nuts

Preheat the oven to 325° F. Grease a 9″ x 5″ x 2 3/4″ loaf pan.

In a large mixing bowl, cream the butter and honey. Add the egg and orange rind and stir until thoroughly blended. Stir in the orange juice.

In a separate bowl, stir together the dry ingredients, then add them to the batter. Stir. Add the nuts and stir to distribute them.

Pour the batter into the greased pan. Bake for 1 hour or until done.

SESAME SEED BREAD
(one large loaf)

2/3 c. raw sugar	1 T. baking powder
1/4 c. liquid oil	3 c. whole wheat flour
2 eggs	1 1/2 c. milk
1 t. grated orange rind	1/2 c. sesame seeds,
1 t. salt	toasted

Preheat the oven to 350° F. Grease a large loaf pan (9″ x 5″ x 2 3/4″).

In a large mixing bowl, stir together the sugar and oil. Beat in the eggs and orange rind.

In a separate bowl, stir together the salt, baking powder, and flour.

Slowly add the flour alternately with the milk to the egg mixture. Stir well after each addition. Finally, add the sesame seeds and stir gently.

Pour the batter into the greased loaf pan. Bake for 50 minutes or until done.

SUNFLOWER LOAF
(one large loaf)

1/2 c. honey	1 T. baking powder
2 T. liquid oil	2 1/4 c. whole wheat flour
1 egg	1 1/4 c. milk
1 T. grated orange rind	3/4 c. sunflower seeds,
1 t. salt	hulled

Preheat the oven to 325° F. Grease a 9″ x 5″ x 2 3/4″ loaf pan.

In a large mixing bowl, stir the honey and oil together. Add the egg and orange rind and beat.

In a separate bowl, combine the salt, baking powder, and flour and stir.

Add the flour mixture alternately with the milk to the honey-egg mixture. Stir well after each addition. Add the sunflower seeds and stir gently.

Pour the batter into the greased pan. Bake for 1 hour or until done.

CARA-NUT BREAD
(one medium loaf)

2 T. butter	1 t. baking powder
3/4 c. raw sugar	1/4 c. carob powder,
2 eggs, beaten	toasted
3/4 c. milk	2 c. whole rye flour
1/2 t. salt	1 c. chopped nuts

Preheat the oven to 350° F. Grease an 8″ x 4″ x 2 3/4″ loaf pan.

In a large mixing bowl, cream the butter and sugar. Add the eggs, milk, and salt, and stir well. Stir in the carob, baking powder, flour, and nuts.

Pour the batter into the greased loaf pan. Bake for 50 minutes or until done.

OAT-NUT BREAD
(one large loaf)

1/3 c. butter	2 t. baking powder
1/4 c. molasses	1 c. rolled oats,
1/4 c. honey	uncooked
2 eggs	1/2 c. nuts, chopped
2/3 c. milk	1/2 t. grated orange rind
1/2 t. salt	2 c. whole wheat flour

Preheat the oven to 325° F. Grease a large loaf pan (9″ x 5″ x 2 3/4″).

Cream the butter, molasses, and honey. Add the eggs and beat well. Stir in the milk, then add the remaining ingredients. Stir well.

Pour into the greased loaf pan. Bake for 1 hour or until done.

PUMPKIN FRUIT CAKE
(one large loaf)

1/4 c. butter	2 T. bran flakes
1/4 c. raw sugar	1 T. grated lemon rind
1/4 c. honey	2 c. whole wheat flour
1 egg	1/2 c. dried fruit, chopped
1 c. pumpkin pureé	(raisins, dates, figs,
1/2 t. salt	apricots, apples, nuts)
2 t. baking powder	

Preheat the oven to 325° F. Grease a 9″ x 5″ x 2 3/4″ loaf pan.

In a large mixing bowl, cream the butter, sugar, and honey. Beat in the egg. Add the pumpkin pureé, salt, baking powder, bran flakes, and lemon rind. Stir until well blended. Stir in the flour, then the dried fruit.

Pour the batter into the greased pan. Bake for 50-60 minutes or until done.

QUICK KUGELHUPF
(one 9" round loaf)

1/4 c. butter	2 t. baking powder
1/3 c. honey	1/2 t. salt
2 eggs	2 1/2 c. whole wheat flour
1 t. grated lemon rind	1 c. milk
1/4 t. nutmeg	1 c. seedless raisins
1/4 t. cinnamon	3-4 T. coarse bran flakes
2 T. soy flour	sliced almonds

Preheat the oven to 350° F. Grease a 9″ tube or Bundt pan. Sprinkle bran flakes on the bottom and sides of the pan. Arrange a handful of almonds on the bottom of the pan.

In a large mixing bowl, cream the butter and honey. Stir in the eggs, lemon rind, nutmeg, cinnamon, and soy flour and mix well.

In a separate bowl, add and stir the baking powder, salt, and flour.

Add the flour to the egg mixture, alternating with the milk. Stir in the raisins.

Pour the batter into the tube pan. Bake for 40 minutes.

QUICK STEAMED BROWN BREAD
(one large loaf or two cans)

1 c. milk	1/2 t. baking powder
1/3 c. molasses	1 1/4 c. whole wheat flour
1/2 t. salt	1/2 c. cornmeal, plain
1/2 t. baking soda	

Grease a large bread pan (9″ x 5″ x 2 3/4″), if a loaf is desired. The cans need not be greased.

Pour enough water into the steamer so that the bread pans will be above water. Heat the water in the steamer.

Stir together the dry ingredients.

In a medium-sized mixing bowl, combine the milk and molasses and stir. Add the dry ingredients and mix well.

Pour the batter into the greased pan or into two No. 303 cans. Carefully place on the steaming racks, cover the pot, and steam for 40-45 minutes over a medium boil.

STREUSEL COFFEE CAKE

1/3 c. raw sugar	Streusel Topping:
1/4 c. liquid oil	2 T. whole wheat flour
1 egg	2 T. butter
2/3 c. milk	1/4 c. raw sugar
1/2 t. vanilla	1 T. grated orange rind
2 T. soy flour	1/4 t. cinnamon
1/2 t. salt	1/4 c. nuts, chopped
1 1/2 t. baking powder	(optional)
2 c. whole wheat flour	

Preheat the oven to 350° F. Grease an 8-inch square pan.

In a small mixing bowl, combine the streusel ingredients and stir with a fork until crumbly.

In a medium-sized mixing bowl, stir the oil and sugar together. Beat in the egg, and add the milk, vanilla, and soy flour. Stir in the flour, baking powder, and salt. Beat until well blended.

Pour the batter into the greased baking pan. Sprinkle the streusel topping over the batter. Bake for 20-25 minutes or until done.

HONEY ALMOND COFFEE CAKE

1/2 c. butter
3/4 c. raw sugar
2 eggs, beaten
1 t. vanilla
3 t. baking powder
1/2 t. salt
2/3 c. milk
2 c. whole wheat flour

Honey Almond Topping:
1/2 c. butter
1/2 c. raw sugar
1/2 c. honey
1/4 t. cinnamon
1/4 c. almonds, slivered
    or sliced

Preheat the oven to 350° F. Butter an 8-inch square pan.

In a large mixing bowl, cream the butter and sugar. Add the eggs, beating them in one at a time. Stir in the vanilla.

In a separate bowl, stir together the dry ingredients. Add the flour mixture alternately with the milk, stirring well after each addition.

Pour the batter into the greased pan. Bake for 30 minutes or until done.

Prepare the topping while the coffee cake is baking. Cream the butter, sugar, honey, and cinnamon. Stir in the almonds.

Spread the topping on the coffee cake as soon as it comes out of the oven.

Return the coffee cake with the topping to the oven for about 5 minutes, or until the topping has melted.

BRAN MUFFINS
(one dozen)

2 c. whole wheat flour
1 T. baking powder
1/2 t. salt
3/4 c. bran flakes
2 T. honey

1 egg
1 c. milk
1/4 c. butter,
    melted and cooled

Preheat the oven to 350° F. Butter the muffin tins.

Stir together the dry ingredients in a mixing bowl.

Beat the honey, egg, milk, and butter in a small bowl. Add the wet ingredients to the dry ingredients. Stir until the dry ingredients are moist, but do not beat.

Fill the muffin tins about 3/4 full. Bake for 20 minutes.

PANCAKES
(serves 2-3)

2 c. whole wheat flour
3 T. raw sugar
1 T. baking powder
1/4 t. salt

2 T. liquid oil
1 egg
1 1/2 c. milk

Heat a lightly greased griddle.

In a medium-sized bowl, stir the flour, sugar, baking powder, and salt. Stir in the oil, egg, and milk.

Pour or spoon the batter into pancakes of desired size onto the hot griddle. Turn the cakes when the bubbles retain their holes.

BREAKFAST PANCAKES
(serves two)

1 3/4 c. warm milk
1 t. dry yeast
1/4 c. honey
1/2 t. salt
1 c. whole wheat flour
1/4 c. whole rye flour

1/4 c. cornmeal, plain
1/4 c. wheat germ
1 t. baking powder
2 T. liquid oil
1 egg, beaten

Dissolve the yeast in the milk, about 5 minutes. Add the honey, salt, wheat and rye flours, cornmeal, and wheat germ. Let stand until bubbly.

Heat a lightly greased griddle.

Add the oil, baking powder and egg to the batter. Stir well.

Pour pancakes of desired size on the hot griddle. Turn the cakes over when the bubbles begin to retain their holes.

CAROB PANCAKES
(serves two)

2 3/4 c. warm milk
1 t. dry yeast
1/4 c. raw sugar
1/2 t. salt
1 1/2 c. whole wheat flour
1/4 c. wheat germ

1/4 c. carob powder,
  toasted
2 T. liquid oil
1 egg, beaten
1 t. baking soda

Dissolve the yeast in the warm milk, about 5 minutes. Add the sugar, salt, flour, wheat germ, and carob powder. Stir and let stand until bubbly.

Heat a lightly greased griddle.

Add the oil, egg, and baking soda to the batter. Stir well.

Pour or spoon silver dollar-size cakes onto the griddle. Turn the cakes when the bubbles begin to retain their holes.

YEAST DOUGHNUTS
(four dozen)

1 T. dry yeast
1 1/4 c. warm milk
1/4 c. raw sugar
1/3 c. butter, melted

1 egg, beaten
1/2 t. salt
3 1/2 c. whole wheat flour

Combine the yeast and milk in a large mixing bowl. Allow the yeast to dissolve, about 5 minutes. Add the remaining ingredients and beat well by hand for 5 minutes. Cover with a clean dish cloth and place in a warm spot to rise.

When the dough has doubled in bulk, punch down, and turn it out onto a well floured board. Sprinkle with a little flour to keep the dough from sticking. Knead gently for a few minutes and shape the dough into a ball. Roll the dough out to about 3/8" to 1/2" thick. Cut with a doughnut cutter. Two drinking glasses may also be used. Use a glass with a 3" diameter to cut the doughnuts from the dough, then use a cordial glass with a 1" diameter to cut the hole out. Remove the holes from the doughnuts.

Place the doughnuts and the holes on a well greased baking sheet to rise. Cover the sheet with a clean dish cloth and place it in a warm place to rise.

When the doughnuts have risen to almost double in bulk, heat peanut oil in a deep fryer to 365° F. Maintain the oil temperature between 365-375° F. Higher temperatures will burn the outside of the doughnuts and leave the center uncooked, and lower temperatures will result in oil-saturated doughnuts.

When the oil is ready for use, dip a spatula in the hot oil, then slip it under one of the doughnuts on the baking sheet to transfer it to the hot oil.

Allow the doughnuts to brown on both sides, then remove them and place them on absorbent paper towels.

BUTTERMILK DOUGHNUTS
(two dozen)

2 eggs	1/2 t. salt
3/4 c. raw sugar	1/4 t. cinnamon
1 c. buttermilk	1/4 t. nutmeg
3 T. butter, melted	4 c. whole wheat flour
1 T. baking powder	

In a large mixing bowl, beat the eggs and sugar. Stir in the remaining ingredients, and mix well.

Cover the bowl and chill the dough in the refrigerator for 30-45 minutes. Chilling makes the dough easier to handle.

After the dough has been chilled, shape it into a ball. Roll it out to about 1/2" thick on a lightly floured board. Cut with a doughnut cutter or two drinking glasses of appropriate sizes. Place on a lightly greased baking sheet until ready to be fried.

Heat peanut oil to 365° F. Maintain the oil temperature between 365-375° F. Higher temperatures will burn the outside of the doughnuts and leave the center uncooked, and lower temperatures will result in oil-soaked doughnuts.

Carefully lift the doughnuts from the baking sheet and place in the hot oil. Do not cook too many doughnuts at one time, since that will lower the temperature of the oil. The doughnuts will sink to the bottom, then rise. Cook for about 2 minutes or until golden brown on both sides.

MALASADAS
(three dozen)

1 1/2 T. dry yeast	4 eggs, beaten
1 1/3 c. warm milk	3 T. butter, melted
1/4 c. raw sugar	3 1/2 c. whole wheat flour
1/2 t. salt	

In a large mixing bowl, combine the yeast and milk. Allow the yeast to dissolve, about 5 minutes. Add the remaining ingredients and beat well. The dough should not be as stiff as bread dough, rather, it should be more of a heavy batter.

Cover the bowl with a clean dish cloth and place it in a warm place to double in bulk.

Heat peanut oil in a deep fryer to 365° F. Maintain the oil temperature between 365° F. and 375° F. A hotter oil will burn the outside of the malasada and leave the center uncooked, and a cooler oil will result in soggy malasadas.

Stir the batter down vigorously, then drop the batter by the heaping tablespoonful into the hot oil. The cooking malasadas will generally turn themselves around in the hot oil. Fry until well browned.

CHAPTER 7

CAKES IN
THE OLD WORLD STYLE

WITH A FEW exceptions, the cakes chosen for this chapter are noted for being delicious by themselves without heavy buttery or sticky sugary icings and fillings. They are usually baked in square or tube pans and may be glazed while still hot (see near end of chapter for glazes) or served with lightly honey-sweetened whipped cream.

Soft wheat or all-purpose flour should be used in cake baking. The crumbly and light texture characteristic of cakes cannot be achieved with a flour having a high gluten content. Like quick breads, cakes rely on baking powder to provide leavening.

Cakes filled with whipped cream must be refrigerated, and are easier to cut and serve when they are prepared, filled, and chilled several hours in advance. Glazed, unfilled cakes, and cheesecakes freeze very well. Allow several hours for them to thaw before serving.

POUND CAKE

1 lb. butter
  (2 cups)
1 lb. raw sugar
  (2 cups)
1 lb. eggs
  (8 large)

1 t. salt
2 t. baking powder
1 t. vanilla extract
1 lb. whole wheat flour
  (4 cups)

Preheat the oven to 325° F. Butter two large loaf pans (9″ x 5″ x 2 3/4″).

Cream the butter and the sugar. Beat well. Add the eggs, beating them in one at a time. Stir in the salt, baking powder, vanilla extract, and flour. Beat vigorously for several minutes.

Pour the batter into the buttered loaf pans. Bake for one hour or until done.

GLAZED YOGURT CAKE

1 c. butter
3/4 c. raw sugar
3 eggs, separated
3/4 c. yogurt
2 T. grated orange rind
2 T. grated lemon or
   grapefruit rind
1/4 t. salt
2 T. soy flour

2 T. coarse bran flakes
2 t. baking powder
2 c. whole rye flour

Honey Glaze:
1/2 c. honey
1 T. orange juice
2 T. lemon juice

Preheat the oven to 350° F. Butter a 9″ tube or Bundt pan.

Cream the butter and beat in the sugar and egg yolks. Stir in the remaining ingredients and beat well.

Beat the egg whites until the peaks hold their shape. Gently fold the egg whites into the cake dough.

Pour the dough into the greased pan. Bake for 35 minutes or until done.

Prepare the glaze by mixing the honey and the juices together before the cake comes out of the oven.

Upon removing the cake from the oven, allow it to cool for about 3 minutes, invert the cake on a plate, and brush all of the glaze over the top and sides.

APPLESAUCE CAKE

1/2 c. butter
3/4 c. raw sugar
1 egg
1/2 t. salt
1 t. baking powder

1 t. cinnamon
1/4 t. nutmeg
2 c. whole wheat flour
1 c. applesauce,
   thick and unsweetened

Preheat the oven to 350° F. Grease and flour an 8″ tube or Bundt pan.

In a large mixing bowl, cream the butter. Beat in the sugar and egg. Stir in the remaining ingredients. Mix well.

Pour the batter into the greased pan. Bake for 50-60 minutes or until done.

CAROB CAKE

1 c. butter	2 T. bran flakes
1/3 c. raw sugar	2 t. baking powder
1/3 c. honey	3 T. carob powder, toasted
3 eggs, separated	2 1/2 c. whole wheat flour
3/4 c. milk or yogurt	1 t. vanilla
1/4 t. salt	1 t. cinnamon

Preheat the oven to 300° F. Butter a 9″ square pan and dust flour over the bottom.

In a large mixing bowl, cream the butter, sugar, and honey. Beat in the egg yolks, milk, salt, bran, baking powder, carob, flour, vanilla, and cinnamon. Beat 4-5 minutes by hand or about 2 minutes with a portable electric mixer.

In a medium-sized bowl, beat the egg whites until stiff. Slowly and gently fold the beaten whites into the batter.

Pour the batter into the greased pan and bake for 30-35 minutes or until done.

PUMPKIN CAKE

1/2 c. butter	1 t. cinnamon
1 c. raw sugar	1/4 t. nutmeg
2 eggs	1 T. baking powder
3/4 c. milk or yogurt	1/4 t. salt
1 c. pumpkin pureé	2 1/4 c. whole wheat flour
1/2 t. ground ginger	

Preheat the oven to 350° F. Grease and flour a 9″ tube pan.

In a large mixing bowl, cream the butter and sugar. Add the eggs, beating in one at a time. Stir in the remaining ingredients in the order listed above. Beat well.

Pour the batter into the tube pan. Bake for 40 minutes or until done.

FRUIT CAKE

2 T. dry yeast
1/2 c. warm water
1/2 c. liquid oil
1/2 c. honey
1 T. grated lemon rind
1/2 t. salt
2 T. soy flour
2 T. bran flakes
2 c. whole rye flour

1 c. nuts, chopped
1 c. raisins
1/2 c. cranberries, chopped
1/2 c. dates, chopped
1/2 c. lemon and/or
    orange peel, chopped
1/2 c. dried figs or
    dates, chopped

Grease a 9" x 5" x 2 3/4" loaf pan.

In a large mixing bowl, combine the yeast and warm water. Allow the yeast to dissolve, about 5 minutes. Stir in the oil, honey, lemon rind, salt, soy flour, and bran flakes. Slowly add the rye flour until the dough pulls away from the side of the bowl. Add the nuts and fruit and allow the dough to rest for 5-10 minutes.

Turn the dough out on a floured board and knead for 5-7 minutes. The dough should be relatively stiff.

Shape the dough and place it in the greased pan. Brush the top with an egg white beaten with 1 T. water. Cover with a clean dish cloth and set in a warm place to rise until about double in bulk.

Preheat the oven to 325° F.

Bake for 50-60 minutes or until done.

OATMEAL CAKE

1 c. rolled oats, uncooked
1 1/2 c. boiling water
1/2 c. butter
1 c. raw sugar
2 eggs

1 t. vanilla
1 1/2 c. whole rye flour
1/2 t. salt
1 t. cinnamon
1 t. baking powder

In a small bowl, pour the boiling water over the oats and allow to cool.

Preheat the oven to 350° F. Grease and flour an 8″ square baking pan.

In a large mixing bowl, cream the butter and sugar. Add the eggs, beating them in one at a time. Stir in the oats and the remaining ingredients. Mix well.

Pour the batter into the baking pan. Bake for 35 minutes or until it tests done.

CARROT CAKE

1 1/2 c. liquid oil	1/2 t. ground cloves
1 3/4 c. raw sugar	2 t. baking powder
4 eggs, separated	2 1/2 c. whole wheat flour
1/4 c. hot water	1 1/2 c. grated
1 t. nutmeg	raw carrots
1 t. cinnamon	1/2 c. raisins

Preheat the oven to 350° F. Grease and flour a 10-inch tube or Bundt pan.

Beat together the oil, sugar, and egg yolks. Add the hot water and stir until the sugar has dissolved. Stir in the spices, baking powder, flour, carrots, and raisins. Mix well.

In a separate bowl, beat the egg whites until stiff, but not dry.

Gently fold the beaten whites into the batter.

Pour the batter into the greased pan.

Bake for 1 hour and 10 minutes or until done.

CARAWAY SEED CAKE

1/2 c. butter	1 T. caraway seeds
1 c. raw sugar	1 T. lemon juice
3 eggs	1/3 c. milk
1/4 t. salt	2 c. whole wheat flour
2 t. baking powder	

Preheat the oven to 350° F. Grease and flour an 8″ tube or Bundt pan.

In a large bowl, cream the butter and sugar. Add the eggs, beating them in one at a time. Stir in the remaining ingredients and mix well.

Pour the batter into the greased tube pan. Bake for 1 hour or until done.

FRESH FRUIT UPSIDE-DOWN CAKE

3 c. fresh fruit, sliced (apples, peaches, apricots, pineapple)	1 egg
	1/2 c. milk
	1 t. grated lemon rind
1/4 c. raw sugar (optional)	1 1/4 c. whole wheat flour
	1 1/2 t. baking powder
1/4 c. butter	1/2 t. salt
2/3 c. raw sugar	

Preheat the oven to 350° F. Butter an 8″ square cake pan.

Arrange the sliced fruit on the bottom of the buttered pan. Sprinkle the 1/4 cup raw sugar over the fruit (optional).

In a large mixing bowl, cream the butter with the sugar. Beat in the egg, then stir in the milk and lemon rind. Add the remaining ingredients and beat for about 5 minutes by hand or 2 minutes with a portable electric beater.

Pour the batter over the fruit in the cake pan. Bake for about 30 minutes. The cake is done when it springs back when lightly pressed with a finger.

GINGERBREAD

1/2 c. butter
1/2 c. raw sugar
1/4 c. molasses
2 eggs
1 1/2 t. baking soda
1 c. milk

1/4 t. salt
2 t. ground ginger
1 t. cinnamon
1/4 t. nutmeg or mace
2 c. whole rye flour
1 t. grated lemon rind

Preheat the oven to 350° F. Grease a 9" square pan and flour its bottom.

In a medium-sized mixing bowl, cream the butter, sugar, and molasses. Beat in the eggs, and add the remaining ingredients. Beat vigorously to blend all ingredients thoroughly.

Pour the batter into the greased pan. Bake for 25 minutes or until it tests done.

SPONGE CAKE

7 eggs, separated
1 c. raw sugar
1 lemon, juice and
  grated rind

1/2 t. salt
1 t. baking powder
1 c. whole wheat flour

Preheat the oven to 325° F.

Beat the egg yolks with the sugar and lemon juice and rind. Stir in the salt, baking powder, and flour and mix well.

In a large bowl, beat the egg whites until stiff, but not dry.

Carefully fold the egg whites into the batter.

Pour the batter into an ungreased 10-inch tube or Bundt pan.

Bake for 1 hour or until done. To cool the cake, invert it and place over an empty oil or wine bottle. When cooled, tap the bottom and sides until the cake is released.

CHINESE STEAMED SPONGE CAKE

1 c. whole wheat flour
1/2 t. baking powder
5 eggs, separated

3/4 c. raw sugar
1 t. lemon extract
1 c. bean filling

To make the bean filling, cook 1/2 cup dried beans (lima, kidney, navy, pinto, etc.) until very soft. Drain the water and put the beans through a blender to pureé. Add honey or raw sugar to sweeten to taste (about 1/2 cup). Allow the filling to cool.

Heat water in a steamer with a tight lid.

Lightly butter an 8-inch square baking pan.

In a medium-sized bowl, beat the egg yolks with the sugar. Add the flour, baking powder, and lemon extract and mix well.

In a separate bowl, beat the egg whites until stiff, but not dry.

Gently fold the egg whites into the batter.

Pour half of the batter into the buttered pan. Gently spread the bean filling over the batter. Pour the remaining batter over the bean filling.

Carefully place the pan on the steaming rack. Steam for 30 minutes over water at a medium boil.

STRAWBERRY CAKE ROLL

3 eggs
3/4 c. raw sugar
1/3 c. water
1 t. grated orange rind
1/2 t. salt

1 t. baking powder
1 c. whole wheat flour
1 qt. fresh strawberries,
  sliced
1 c. heavy cream

Preheat the oven to 350° F. Grease a 15″ x 10″ pan and line the bottom with waxed paper.

Beat the eggs with the sugar. Stir in the water, orange rind, salt, baking powder, and flour. Beat well.

Pour the batter into the lined pan. Bake for 10-15 minutes or until done.

Upon removing the pan from the oven, turn the cake out on a clean, dry dish cloth. Peel off the waxed paper. Roll the cake in the towel to form a 15-inch cylinder. Allow the cake to cool in the towel.

Whip the cream, sweetening it with honey, if desired.

Unroll the cake when it has cooled. Spread the whipped cream and strawberries over it. Reroll and refrigerate.

FRESH STRAWBERRY TORTE

1/3 c. butter
3 T. raw sugar
1/2 t. grated lemon rind
1/3 c. grated nuts,
   preferably almonds
1/2 c. whole wheat flour
1 qt. fresh strawberries,
   hulled

1 c. mashed strawberries
1 c. water
1/3 c. honey
1 T. lemon juice
1 pkg. gelatin

Preheat the oven to 300° F.

Cream the butter and sugar. Add the lemon rind, grated nuts, and flour. Stir well.

Press the dough onto the bottom of a 10″ spring form pan or a 9″ pie plate, forming a rim of about 1/2″ to 3/4″.

Bake for 20 minutes. Allow to cool thoroughly in the pan.

Prepare the topping. If the strawberries are large, slice them in half. Small strawberries may be used whole. Arrange the strawberries on the torte base.

Combine the remaining ingredients in a saucepan and heat until the gelatin is thoroughly dissolved. Remove from the heat and cool, but do not allow the mixture to congeal. If it does congeal, it may be heated again to liquefy. Pour the gel over the base and refrigerate to set the gel. Keep refrigerated until serving.

STRAWBERRY MERINGUE CAKE

1/2 c. butter
1/3 c. honey
3 eggs, separated
1 t. baking powder
1/2 c. milk
1 c. whole wheat flour

3/4 c. raw sugar,
    ground to a powder
1 oz. sliced almonds
1 c. whipping cream
1 pt. fresh strawberries,
    hulled

Preheat the oven to 350° F. Butter and flour one 9" cake pan.

In a medium-sized mixing bowl, cream the butter and honey. Add the egg yolks, baking powder, milk, and flour. Beat for 2 minutes.

Pour the batter into the greased pan. Bake for 30 minutes or until done. Allow to cool thoroughly.

Beat the egg whites until stiff. Add the powdered sugar and beat to blend in. Turn the beatened whites out on a 9" cake pan. Sprinkle with the sliced almonds. Bake the meringue at 300° F. for about 2 hours. Allow the meringue to cool slowly in the oven. Do not open the oven door for at least 3 hours while it is cooling. (The meringue may be made up in advance, providing the humidity is low.)

Whip the cream, sweetening it, if desired, with honey.

Turn the cake out onto a cake plate. Spread half the whipped cream over the cake. Arrange fresh strawberries over the whipped cream. Cover with the remaining whipped cream. Top the cake with the cooled and crisp meringue. Serve immediately.

BLITZ TORTE

1/4 lb. butter
1/2 c. raw sugar
4 eggs, separated
pinch of salt
2 t. baking powder
1/2 t. vanilla
4 T. milk

3/4 c. whole wheat flour
2 oz. sliced almonds
1 c. raw sugar, powdered
pinch of cream of tartar
1 c. heavy cream
1 T. honey

Preheat th oven to 325° F. Line two 8″ cake pans with waxed paper.

Cream the butter and add the sugar with a pinch of salt. Stir in the egg yolks and the vanilla. Add the baking powder, milk, and flour. Beat well.

Spread an equal amount of dough in each of the cake pans.

In a medium-sized bowl, beat the egg whites until stiff. Add 1 c. powdered raw sugar with a pinch of cream of tartar. Beat until well blended.

Divide the beaten whites into each of the cake pans and spread over the dough. Sprinkle the tops with sliced almonds.

Bake for 30 minutes or until meringue is a light brown.

Allow the cakes to cool before removing them from the pans. Invert one cake layer on a plate and remove the waxed paper.

Beat the heavy cream with 1 T. honey.

Spread the whipped cream on the bottom layer. Carefully lift the remaining layer from its pan, remove its waxed paper, and set it in place over the whipped cream.

Refrigerate the cake. Blitz torte is best prepared and refrigerated for several hours before serving.

(*Note:* Do not substitute honey for sugar in the meringue or cake dough.)

KUGELHUPF

1 T. dry yeast	2 c. whole wheat flour
3/4 c. warm water	2/3 c. raisins
1/3 c. honey	1 t. grated lemon rind
1/2 t. salt	1/4 t. nutmeg
1/4 c. butter	3-4 T. coarse bran flakes
3 T. milk powder	whole or sliced almonds
2 eggs	

In a large mixing bowl, combine the yeast and water. Allow the yeast to dissolve, about 5 minutes. Add the honey, salt, butter, milk powder, eggs, and flour, and beat well.

Cover with a clean dish cloth and allow to rise in a warm place until double in bulk.

Grease a 9" tube or Bundt pan. Sprinkle bran flakes in the pan until the sides and bottom are well coated. Arrange the almonds on the bottom.

Preheat the oven to 350° F.

Beat the batter thoroughly, add raisins, grated lemon rind, and nutmeg. Stir well.

Pour the batter into the prepared tube pan. Let the batter rise again until double in bulk. Bake for 45-50 minutes or until done.

CHEESECAKE

1/2 c. bran flakes	3/4 c. honey
1 1/2 lb. cream cheese	3 T. lemon juice
3 eggs	1 T. lemon rind
1/2 c. raw sugar	1 pt. strawberries, fresh or frozen

Preheat the oven to 300° F. Butter an 8" spring form pan or souffle dish. Sprinkle bran flakes in the pan until the sides and bottom are coated.

Cream the cheese and beat in the eggs, sugar, honey, lemon juice, and grated rind. Beat, preferably with an electric beater, until the batter is smooth and light.

Pour the batter into the prepared pan.

Place the pan in a larger pan of hot water in the oven. Bake for 1 1/2 hours. Allow the cheesecake to cool slowly in the oven with the door closed for about 30 minutes. Remove from the oven and allow it to complete its cooling on a cake rack.

Top with strawberries just before serving.

HONEY LEMON GLAZE

1/3 c. honey
3 T. fresh lemon juice

Stir the honey and lemon juice together. Brush onto hot cake.

CITRUS GLAZE

1/2 c. raw sugar
2 T. fresh lemon juice
2 T. fresh orange or grapefruit juice

Dissolve over low heat before brushing on the hot cake.

CHAPTER 8

THE JOY OF COOKIES

COOKIES ARE PERHAPS the simplest of the baked goods to prepare and the quickest to bake, often requiring only 15-20 minutes from the start to the munch. Possibilities for varying cookie recipes are vast, and a favorite flavoring, fruit, nut, or nutritional supplement may be added with little or no change to the rest of the recipe.

Whole wheat or rye flour may be used interchangeably in all of the cookie recipes. Whole rye flour imparts an especially nutty flavor and is particularly pleasing in cookies. Soy flour is used in many of the cookie recipes as a protein supplement. Either high fat or low fat flour may be used. In cookie recipes where soy flour is not called for, 10-25% of the wheat or rye flour may be substituted by soy flour. When adding soy flour to a recipe, remember that soy flour tends to make cookies brown faster. Either a slightly lower oven temperature or a shorter baking time may be required.

COOKIE STORAGE

Storage of cookies is largely determined by two factors: 1) whether the cookie is soft or crisp and 2) the humidity of the air. Cookies that are crisp are baked with a large amount of butter or liquid oil, and very little or no other liquid. They stay crisp in low humidity, but absorb moisture and get soft in high humidity. Soft cookies, conversely, dry out in low humidity and remain soft in high humidity.

Cookbooks usually direct that soft cookies be kept in airtight containers and crisp cookies in loose lidded ones. If cookies are to be stored over a period of time, however, it is best to store all cookies, crisp or soft, in airtight containers. If storage is for a short time only, airtight containers are necessary only for crisp cookies in high humidit or soft cookies for low humidity. For long term storage, freezing cookies is recommended. Cookies may be packed in small plastic bags and tied tightly. Coffee cans with plastic lids are also good for airtight freezing.

BUTTER COOKIES
(40 crisp cookies)

2/3 c. butter
1/2 c. raw sugar
1 egg, separated
1/4 t. salt

1/4 c. milk
1 1/4 c. whole wheat flour
poppy seeds, sesame seeds, or
finely chopped nuts for topping

In a large mixing bowl, beat the butter, sugar, and egg yolk until smooth and creamy. Add the salt, milk, and flour and stir well.

Refrigerate the dough for about one hour or until the dough becomes hard enough to handle.

Preheat the oven to 325° F.

In a small dish, beat the egg white with 1 T. water.

Divide the dough into 3 parts. Shape each part into a ball. Return two balls to the refrigerator and roll out the remaining ball on a floured board until about 1/8″ thick. Cut out the dough with a round cookie cutter or a drinking glass with a 2″ diameter. Place each cookie round on an ungreased cookie sheet.

Brush each cookie with the beaten egg white, then sprinkle the top with seeds or chopped nuts. Bake for 10 minutes or until lightly browned.

RYE SHORTBREAD
(about 20 bars)

1 c. butter
1/2 c. raw sugar
2 1/2 c. whole rye flour

Preheat the oven to 325° F.

Cream the butter and sugar until the sugar has dissolved. Add the rye flour and stir well.

Press the dough firmly into a 9 x 9″ baking pan.

Bake for 30 minutes. Cut into bars while hot.

DATE-OATMEAL COOKIES
(60 crisp cookies)

3/4 c. butter
1 c. raw sugar
1 egg
1/4 c. water
1 t. vanilla

1 t. salt
1/2 t. baking powder
1 c. whole wheat flour
3 c. rolled oats, uncooked
1 1/2 c. dates, chopped finely

Preheat oven to 350° F. Grease cookie sheets.

In a large mixing bowl, beat butter, sugar, egg, water, vanilla, and salt until thoroughly mixed. Stir in the baking powder and flour, and mix well. Add the oats and chopped dates.

Drop dough by the heaping teaspoonful onto cookie sheet and bake for 10-12 minutes or until golden brown at the edges.

OATMEAL NUGGETS
(40 crisp cookies)

1 1/2 c. rolled oats, raw
1/3 c. raw sugar
3 T. molasses
1/2 c. liquid oil
1 egg
1 t. salt

2/3 c. whole rye flour
1 t. baking powder
2 T. soy flour
2 T. wheat germ
1/2 c. chopped nuts

Preheat the oven to 350° F. Grease two cookie sheets.

In a large mixing bowl, combine oats, sugar, molasses, oil, egg, and salt. Stir well and add whole rye flour, baking powder, soy flour, wheat germ, and chopped nuts.

Drop by the heaping teaspoonful onto a cookie sheet and bake for about 10 minutes. Let the cookies cool slightly before removing them from the cookie sheets onto cooling racks.

OAT-NUTS
(40 crisp cookies)

1 c. rolled oats, raw
3/4 c. raw sugar
1/2 c. liquid oil
1 egg
1 t. salt

2/3 c. whole rye flour
2 T. soy flour
1 t. baking powder
1/2 c. nuts, chopped

Preheat the oven to 375° F. Grease two cookie sheets.

In a large mixing bowl, combine oats, sugar, oil, egg, and salt. Stir in the rye flour, soy flour, baking powder, and chopped nuts.

Drop the dough by the teaspoonful onto cookie sheet. These cookies do not spread very much so they may be placed relatively close to each other during baking. Bake for 8-10 minutes. Let the cookies cool slightly before removing them from the cookie sheets.

LACY OATMEAL COOKIES
(40 crisp cookies)

1 1/2 c. rolled oats, raw	1 t. salt
3/4 c. raw sugar	1 t. baking powder
2/3 c. liquid oil	1/2 c. whole wheat flour
1 egg	1/2 c. chopped nuts

Preheat the oven to 375° F. Grease two cookie sheets.

In a large mixing bowl, combine the oats, sugar, liquid oil, egg, and salt. Stir well. Add baking powder, whole wheat flour, and nuts and mix well.

Drop by the teaspoonful onto cookie sheet. Bake for 7-8 minutes or until golden brown at the edges. Let the cookies cool slightly before removing them from the cookie sheets onto a cooling rack.

CAROB COOKIES
(40 chewy cookies)

1/2 c. butter	1/4 c. soy flour
3/4 c. raw sugar	1 t. baking powder
1 egg	1/4 c. carob powder
2 T. molasses	1/4 t. cinnamon
1 1/2 c. whole rye flour	

Preheat the oven to 350° F. Grease two cookie sheets.

In a medium-sized mixing bowl, cream the butter and sugar. Add the egg and molasses and beat. Stir in the remaining dry ingredients and mix thoroughly.

Drop by the teaspoonful onto the greased cookie sheets. Bake for 8-10 minutes.

POPPY SEED COOKIES
(30 crisp cookies)

1/2 c. liquid oil
1/2 c. raw sugar
1 egg
1 T. soy flour
1 T. milk powder

1 t. salt
1 t. baking powder
1 T. poppy seeds
1 c. whole rye flour

Preheat the oven to 350° F. Grease two cookie sheets.

In a medium-sized mixing bowl, beat together the oil, sugar, and egg. Stir in the remaining ingredients and mix well.

Form into balls about 3/4" in diameter. Place the balls about 3" apart on the cookie sheet and flatten them until about 1/4" thick.

Bake for 7 minutes or until brown around the edges.

MOLASSES COOKIES
(36 crisp cookies)

1/2 c. liquid oil
1/4 c. raw sugar
3/4 c. molasses
1 egg
3 T. milk powder

1/2 t. salt
1 t. ginger
1 t. cinnamon
2 T. soy flour
2 c. whole rye flour

Preheat the oven to 350° F. Grease two cookie sheets.

In a large mixing bowl, beat oil, sugar, molasses, and egg. Stir in the remaining ingredients and mix thoroughly.

Form the dough into balls about 3/4" in diameter. Place the balls about 3" apart on the cookie sheet and flatten the balls until they are about 1/4" thick.

Bake for 8-10 minutes.

DATE NUTTIES
(30 crisp cookies)

1/2 c. liquid oil	1/2 t. salt
1/2 c. raw sugar	1 t. baking powder
1 egg	1 c. whole rye flour
3 T. soy flour	1/2 c. chopped nuts
1 T. bran flakes	1/2 c. chopped dates

Preheat the oven to 350° F. Grease two cookie sheets.

In a medium-sized mixing bowl, beat together the oil, sugar, and egg. Stir in the remaining ingredients and mix thoroughly.

Form the dough into balls about 3/4" in diameter. Place them about 3" apart on a cookie sheet and flatten them until about 1/4" thick.

Bake for 8-10 minutes or until lightly browned.

HI-SOY COOKIES
(36 crisp cookies)

2/3 c. butter	1/2 t. salt
2/3 c. sugar	1/3 c. soy flour
1 egg	1 t. baking powder
1 T. grated orange rind	1 1/2 c. whole rye flour

Preheat the oven to 350° F. Grease two cookie sheets.

In a medium-sized mixing bowl, cream the butter and sugar. Beat in the egg and orange rind. Stir in the dry ingredients.

Form the dough into balls about 1" in diameter. Place the balls on cookie sheets about 3" apart, and flatten the dough until about 1/4" thick.

Bake for 5 minutes or until golden brown.

SUNSHINE COOKIES
(two dozen crisp cookies)

1/2 c. liquid oil
1/3 c. raw sugar
1 egg
1/2 t. salt
1 t. baking powder
2 T. soy flour
1 1/3 c. whole rye flour

1 T. poppy seed
1 T. sesame seeds,
  raw or toasted
1 T. alfalfa seeds
1 T. anise seeds
2 T. sunflower seeds

Preheat the oven to 350° F. Grease two cookie sheets.

In a medium-sized mixing bowl, stir oil, sugar, and egg together. Mix in the remaining ingredients.

Shape the dough into balls about 1″ in diameter. Place them about 3″ apart on a cookie sheet. Flatten the balls about 1/4″ thick.

Bake for 12-15 minutes.

ALMOND RICE COOKIES
(two dozen crisp cookies)

1/2 c. liquid oil
1/2 c. raw sugar
1 egg
1 t. pure almond extract
1/4 t. salt

1 t. baking powder
2 T. soy flour
3/4 c. brown rice flour
3/4 c. whole rye flour

Preheat oven to 350° F. Grease one cookie sheet.

In a large mixing bowl beat the oil, sugar, egg, and almond extract. Stir in the remaining ingredients. Mix well.

Shape the dough into balls about 1″ in diameter and place on cookie sheet about 3″ apart. Flatten the balls to about 1/4″ thick.

Bake for 10-12 minutes or until lightly browned.

PEANUT COOKIES
(three dozen crisp cookies)

1/2 c. liquid oil	2 T. soy flour
1/2 c. raw sugar	1 t. baking powder
1 egg	1 1/2 c. chopped peanuts (raw)
1/2 t. salt	1 c. whole rye flour

Preheat oven to 350° F. Grease two cookie sheets.

In a medium-sized mixing bowl, beat oil, sugar, and egg. Stir in the remaining ingredients. Mix well.

Form the dough into balls about 1″ in diameter and place on cookie sheets about 2″ apart. Flatten to about 1/4″ thick.

Bake for 10-12 minutes or until golden brown.

YOGURT DROPS
(about 60 soft cookies)

1/2 c. liquid oil	1 c. yogurt, plain
1 c. raw sugar	1 t. baking powder
2 eggs	3 c. whole rye flour
1/2 t. salt	1 T. grated orange rind

Preheat oven to 350° F. Grease two cookie sheets.

In a large mixing bowl, beat the oil sugar, and eggs. Stir in the remaining ingredients and mix well.

Drop dough by the tablespoonful onto the cookie sheets, about 1 1/2″ apart.

Bake for 10-12 minutes or until lightly browned.

BRAN GERM COOKIES
(two dozen crisp cookies)

1/2 c. liquid oil
1/2 c. raw sugar
1 egg
1/2 t. salt
1 T. lemon rind

1 T. soy flour
1 t. baking powder
1/2 c. bran flakes
   and wheat germ
2/3 c. whole rye flour

Preheat the oven to 350° F. Grease a cookie sheet.

In a medium-sized mixing bowl, beat the oil, sugar, and egg. Stir in the remaining ingredients. Mix well.

Form dough into balls about 1″ in diameter. Place on cookie sheet about 2″ apart. Flatten dough until about 1/4″ thick.

Bake 12-15 minutes or until golden brown.

FILLED COOKIES
(about 10 crisp 4″ cookies)

1/2 c. liquid oil
1/2 c. raw sugar
1 egg
1/2 t. salt
2 T. soy flour
2 T. milk powder
1 t. baking powder
1 1/2 c. whole rye flour

Filling:
2 T. dates, chopped
2 T. seedless raisins
3 T. nuts, chopped
1 T. sesame seeds,
   raw or toasted
2 T. honey

Preheat the oven to 350° F. Grease one cookie sheet.

In a small mixing bowl, stir together all ingredients for the filling.

In a medium-sized mixing bowl, beat the oil, sugar, and egg together. Stir in the remaining ingredients.

Form the dough into balls about 1 1/2″ in diameter. Place the balls on the cookie sheet about 4-5″ apart. Flatten the balls of dough until about 3/8″ thick. With the thumb or the bottom of a tablespoon, make a slight indentation in the center of each cookie. Place a teaspoonful of filling in the indentation.

Bake for 10 minutes or until lightly browned.

Filled cookies.

FRUIT BARS

1/4 c. liquid oil	1/2 t. ginger, powdered
3 T. honey	2 T. soy flour
1/4 c. molasses	1 c. whole rye flour
2 eggs	1 c. raisins
1 T. grated orange rind	1/2 c. nuts, chopped
1/2 t. salt	1/2 c. dates, chopped
2 t. baking powder	1/2 c. bananas, mashed

Preheat the oven to 325° F. Grease a 9-inch square pan.

In a large mixing bowl, beat the oil, honey, molasses, and eggs. Stir in the remaining ingredients and mix well.

Pour the batter into the baking pan and bake for 25 minutes or until done. Cut into bars of desired size.

FIG BARS

1/4 c. liquid oil	2 T. soy flour
1/2 c. raw sugar	1/2 t. salt
1 egg	1 t. baking powder
1/3 c. milk	2 c. whole wheat flour
1 t. pure vanilla extract	2 c. dried figs, chopped

Preheat oven to 350° F. Grease an 8-inch square pan.

Beat together oil, sugar, egg, milk, and vanilla. Stir in the soy flour, salt, baking powder, and whole wheat flour. Mix well.

Spread half of the batter in the baking pan. Sprinkle all of the chopped figs over the batter. Spread the remaining half of the dough over the figs.

Bake for 20 minutes or until done. Cut into bars of desired size.

OATMEAL BARS

1/3 c. liquid oil	2 t. baking powder
3/4 c. raw sugar	1/2 c. toasted wheat germ
2 T. molasses	2 c. rolled oats,
1 egg	uncooked
1 t. salt	2 c. whole wheat flour
1 c. milk	1 c. raisins

Preheat the oven to 350° F. Grease a 7" x 11" baking pan.

In a large mixing bowl, stir together the oil, sugar, molasses, egg, and salt. Add the remaining ingredients in the order listed above, stirring after each addition.

Pour the batter into the baking pan and bake for 30 minutes or until done. Allow to cool before cutting into desired size.

PEANUTTIE BARS

2 T. liquid oil	1 T. baking powder
1/4 c. honey	1 c. peanut flour
1/4 c. raw sugar	(raw or toasted)
2 eggs	1 c. whole rye flour
1 t. salt	

Preheat the oven to 325° F. Lightly grease an 8-inch square pan.

In a medium-sized bowl, stir together the oil, honey, and sugar. Add the eggs, beating them in one at a time. Stir in the remaining dry ingredients and mix well.

Pour the thick batter into the square pan and bake for 25 minutes or until done. Allow to cool, then cut into bars of desired size.

CAROB BROWNIES

1/2 c. liquid oil	1 c. whole wheat flour
1/2 c. raw sugar	2 T. soy flour
1/4 c. molasses	1/4 t. salt
1 egg	1 1/2 t. baking powder
2 T. toasted carob powder	1/2 c. chopped nuts

Preheat the oven to 300° F. Grease an 8-inch square pan.

In a medium-sized mixing bowl, combine oil, sugar, molasses, and egg and stir well. Add the remaining ingredients and stir until well blended.

Spread the batter in the greased pan. Bake for 25 minutes or until done. Cut into desired size while the brownies are still warm.

PFLAUMENKUCHEN
(Plum Bars)

2 T. butter
2 T. sugar
1 egg
1/3 c. milk
1 t. lemon rind, grated

1 t. baking powder
1/4 t. salt
1 c. whole wheat flour
3 c. ripe plums, pitted and
    cut into halves or quarters

Preheat oven to 325° F. Butter an 11″ x 7″ baking pan.

In a medium-sized mixing bowl, cream the butter and sugar and beat in the egg. Stir in the milk and lemon rind. Add the remaining ingredients and mix well.

Spread the dough in the baking pan. Arrange plum pieces on the dough. Sprinkle the plums with a little sugar (optional).

Bake for 20 minutes or until done. Cut into bars of desired size.

CHAPTER 9

SURE WAYS
WITH PIES AND PUDDINGS

COMPLAINTS ARE OFTEN heard from home bakers that they would bake pies more often if the crust didn't have to be prepared. It is true that preparing the crust can take as long or longer than preparing the filling, but single pie shells can also be prepared in advance and frozen. It is almost as easy to prepare several pie shells at one time as it is to make one. The shells can be stacked, separated by a sheet of waxed paper, one on top of the other and placed in a plastic bag. To use the frozen shells, allow them 20-30 minutes to thaw and proceed as usual.

Pie pastry should be made with all purpose or pastry flour, a low gluten flour. Shortening and water are literally cut into the flour with a pastry blender or two knives. This ensures that the heat of the baker's hands does not melt the shortening and that the gluten will not be developed, thus producing a flaky product. The pie pastry should be refrigerated before being rolled out because the chilled dough is easier to handle.

Before rolling the chilled dough out, divide it into single pie portions. Shape each portion into a ball. Flatten a ball with the hands and

place on a floured board. Using a rolling pin, roll the dough from the center out to the edges. Roll the dough into a circle large enough so that it is about 1 inch larger than the pie pan. Place the rolled pastry in the pan in either of two ways: 1) Fold the dough in half, lift it, place it in half of the pan, then unfold the other half to cover the pan completely. 2) Place the rolling pin at the edge of the dough and roll the dough around it. Unroll the dough over the pie pan and settle it in place.

The rim of the crust can be made in different ways, according to whether a high or low rim is desired. The edge of the dough should be trimmed to about 1/2 inch from the rim of the pan. To form the rim, roll the overlapping dough under towards the outside. The rim may be left plain as it is or it may be fluted. To flute, position the thumb and forefinger of the left hand on the inside of the rim.

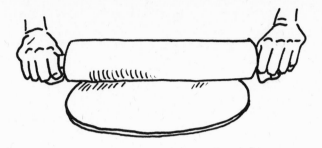

Making pie crusts—rolling the dough from the center out to the edges.

Unrolling the dough over the pie pan and settling it in place.

Forming a fluted rim.

With the forefinger of the right hand on the outside of the rim, press the dough between the two fingers of the left hand. Repeat until the entire rim is fluted. To make a low rim, flatten it with a fork.

If a pie shell is to be baked before it is filled, prick the bottom and sides with a fork to allow steam and air to escape during baking. The pie shell will tend to get bubbly and shrink more if it is not pricked. Lightly brush the bottom and sides with a beatened egg white to help retain the flakiness after it is filled. Bake the shell for about 15 minutes at 425° F. or until it is lightly browned.

Some of the pie fillings—pumpkin, custard—can be baked in a smaller and deeper dish without the crust. Some of the puddings—persimmon, orange custard—on the other hand, also make delicious pie fillings.

BASIC WHOLE WHEAT PIE CRUST
(1-9" double or 2 single crusts)

> 2 c. whole wheat flour
> 1/2 t. salt
> 2/3 c. lard
> 3-5 T. cold water

In a medium-sized bowl, stir together the flour and salt. Blend in the lard with a pastry blender or two knives. Slowly add as much of the water as necessary to make the dough stick together. The dough should not feel wet and sticky.

Cover the dough and place in the refrigerator for at least one hour to chill. This will make the dough easier to handle.

Divide the dough equally in two. Shape into balls, then roll out for two single or one double crust.

RYE PIE CRUST
(1-9" double or 2 single crusts)

1 c. whole wheat flour
1 c. whole rye flour
1 t. salt

1/4 c. cold water
2/3 c. lard

In a medium-sized mixing bowl, stir together the flours and salt. Blend in the lard with a pastry blender or two knives. Slowly add as much of the water as necessary. The dough should barely stick together, and should not be wet and sticky.

Cover and place the pie crust dough in the refrigerator for at least one hour to chill. This will make the dough easier to handle.

Divide the dough into two equal parts, shape into balls, and roll out for two single or one double crust.

LIQUID OIL PIE CRUST
(2-9" single crusts)

2 1/4 c. whole wheat flour
1/2 t. salt
1/2 c. liquid oil
1 1/2 T. cold water or milk

In a medium-sized bowl, stir together the flour and salt. Stir in the liquid oil and cold water. The dough will be moister than other pie crust doughs which are rolled out.

Divide the dough into two parts. Press each part onto a 9" pie pan, forming a ridge at the top. This dough should not be used with a recipe calling for a double crust.

SOY PIE CRUST
(1-9" single crust)

1 c. whole wheat flour
2 T. soy flour
1/4 t. salt

1/3 c. lard
3-4 T. cold water

In a medium-sized mixing bowl, stir together the flours and salt. Blend in the lard with a pastry blender or two knives. Slowly add as much of the water as necessary. The dough should barely stick together, and should not be wet and sticky.

Cover and place the pie crust dough in the refrigerator for at least one hour to chill. This will make the dough easier to handle.

Shape the dough into a ball and roll out.

BUTTER CRUST
(1-9" single crust)

1 c. whole wheat flour
1/4 t. salt
1/3 c. butter
1-2 T. cold water

In a medium-sized bowl, stir together the flour and salt. (Do not use salt if the butter is already salted.) Blend in the butter with a pastry blender or two knives. Stir in only as much water as necessary to make the dough stick together. The dough should not feel wet and sticky.

Cover the bowl and place in the refrigerator for about one hour to chill. Chilling makes the dough easier to handle.

Shape the dough into a ball and roll out. Place on a 9" pie pan and form a fluted rim.

SHORTBREAD CRUST
(1-9" single crust)

1 c. whole wheat flour
3 T. raw sugar
1/3 c. butter

Combine all ingredients and blend well.

Press the dough onto a pie pan, forming a ridge at the rim of the pan.

Bake for 10 minutes at 325° F. or until lightly browned.

(Note: This pie pastry is best used with fresh fruit pies.)

FRUIT PIE

1-9" unbaked pie shell
  (double crust)
5-6 c. fresh apples,
  peaches, or cherries
1/3-2/3 c. raw sugar,
  depending on the tartness
  of the fruit

1/4 t. salt
1 T. whole wheat flour
1/2 t. grated lemon rind
1 t. lemon juice

Preheat the oven to 350° F.

Peel and slice the apples or peaches. Pit the cherries.

In a large bowl, gently stir together the fruit, sugar, salt, flour, lemon rind, and lemon juice. Adjust the ingredients to taste, depending on the tartness of the fruit.

Neatly arrange the fruit in the pie shell. Cover with the upper crust and seal the upper and lower crusts. With a knife or fork, cut openings in the top crust to allow air to escape during baking.

Bake for 50-60 minutes or until crust is a light golden brown.

FRESH FRUIT PIE

1-9″ baked pie shell
  (butter crust preferred)
5-6 c. fresh whole and
  hulled strawberries
  or sliced peaches

1/4 c. honey
1 c. heavy cream

Gently stir the fruit with honey. Chill.

Just before serving, pour the chilled fruit into the pie shell. Whip the cream and spread over the fruit. The cream may be sweetened with honey.

BASIC CUSTARD PIE

1-9″ unbaked pie shell
3 eggs
1/3 c. honey

2 c. milk
1 t. vanilla
1/4 t. salt

Preheat the oven to 450° F. Brush the unbaked pie shell with a beaten egg white to prevent the crust from later becoming soggy. Partially bake the pie shell for about 5 minutes. Remove the pie shell from the oven and allow it to cool. Reduce the oven temperature to 325° F.

Beat the eggs in a medium-sized bowl. Stir in the honey, milk, vanilla, and salt. Pour the mixture into the cooled pie shell.

Bake for 30 minutes or until a knife inserted in the center of the pie comes out clean. Serve warm or chilled.

CAROB CREAM PIE

1-9″ baked pie shell
2 T. cornstarch
1/3 c. raw sugar
1/4 t. salt
3 T. carob powder, toasted

1/4 t. cinnamon
2 c. milk
2 eggs; separated
1 t. vanilla

Stir together the dry ingredients in the top of a double boiler. Add the milk and stir until completely blended. Cook the mixture over boiling water, stirring constantly, until it thickens, about 10 minutes.

In a small dish, beat the egg yolks lightly. Stir the yolks into the hot mixture. Cook for 2 more minutes, stirring constantly. Remove from the heat and cool slightly.

Stir in the vanilla and allow to cool.

Preheat the oven to 325° F.

Beat the egg whites until stiff. Sugar or honey may be added to sweeten the meringue. Spread the meringue over the top of the pie.

Bake for 5 minutes or until the meringue is lightly browned.

PUMPKIN PIE

1-9″ unbaked single pie shell
1 1/2 c. pumpkin pureé
   (or winter squash pureé)
4 T. whole wheat flour
2 eggs, beaten
1 1/2 c. milk or cream
1/3 c. raw sugar

1/4 c. honey
1/2 t. salt
1 t. cinnamon
1/2 t. ginger, powdered
1/4 t. nutmeg
1/8 t. mace

Preheat the oven to 325° F.

In a large mixing bowl, combine all the ingredients in the order listed above. Stir well.

Pour the filling into the unbaked pie shell and bake for 50 minutes or until a knife inserted into the center of the pie comes out clean.

LEMON MERINGUE PIE

1-8" baked pie shell
1 c. raw sugar
1 1/4 c. warm water
1 T. butter
1/4 c. cornstarch

3 T. cold water
3 eggs, separated
3 T. milk
1/3 c. fresh lemon juice

In a 2-quart saucepan, combine the sugar, warm water, and butter. Heat and stir until the sugar has dissolved. Stir the cornstarch with the cold water and add to the saucepan. Cook over low heat for 8-10 minutes, or until the cornstarch has cooked. Beat the egg yolks with the milk and slowly add to the cooking mixture. Cook an additional 2 minutes, stirring constantly.

Remove from the heat and add the lemon juice. Cool. Pour the filling into the cool pie shell.

Preheat the oven to 325° F.

Prepare the meringue by beating the egg whites until stiff. Sweeten with a little honey and beat to blend it in.

Cover the lemon filling with the meringue.

Bake for 5 minutes or until the meringue is lightly browned.

BANANA CREAM PIE

1-9" baked pie shell
2 large bananas
1/3 c. raw sugar
1/4 t. salt

3 T. cornstarch
2 c. milk
2 eggs, well beaten
1 t. grated lemon rind

In a 3-quart saucepan, stir together the sugar, salt, and cornstarch. Add the milk and stir well. Place over medium low heat and stirring constantly, cook until the mixture thickens (about 10 minutes). Remove from the heat and continuing to stir, add the eggs. Return to the stove and cook an additional 5 minutes over a low flame. Continue to stir while the mixture is cooking. Remove from the heat, add the grated lemon rind, and allow to cool slightly.

Place a layer of sliced bananas over the bottom of the pie shell. Pour half of the cream filling over the bananas. Place another layer of sliced bananas over the filling. Finally, pour the remaining filling over the bananas. Allow to cool, then place in the refrigerator to chill before serving.

PECAN PIE

1-9″ unbaked single
  pie shell
1/4 c. butter
1 c. raw sugar
3 eggs

1/4 c. honey
1 t. lemon juice
1/2 t. salt
1 c. pecans, chopped
pecan halves

Preheat the oven to 350° F.

In a medium-sized bowl, cream the butter and sugar. Add the eggs, beating in one at a time. Stir in the honey, lemon juice, salt, and chopped pecans.

Pour the filling into the pie shell. Arrange the pecan halves decoratively over the top of the filling.

Bake for 50 minutes or until done. The pie may be tested by inserting a knife into its center. A clean knife indicates that the pie is done. Serve warm or cold.

RAISIN PIE

1-9″ pie shell, baked
1/4 c. raw sugar
1/2 t. salt
6 T. whole wheat flour
2 c. milk

2 T. honey
2 eggs, separated
2 T. lemon juice
3/4 c. raisins
1/4 c. pecans, chopped

Stir the sugar, salt, and flour in a 3-quart saucepan. Stir in the honey and milk and heat under a medium flame. Add the egg yolks, lemon juice, and raisins. Stir until the mixture thickens, about 7 minutes. Remove from the heat, add the pecans, and let cool slightly. Pour the filling into the baked pie shell.

Preheat the oven to 350° F.

To make the meringue, beat the egg whites until stiff. Add sugar or honey to sweeten, if desired.

Spread the meringue over the filling. Bake for 5 minutes, or until the meringue is a light brown.

GRAPE PIE

4 c. red grapes	1 T. lemon juice
1 c. raw sugar	1 T. butter
3-4 T. whole wheat flour	pie pastry dough
1 /2 t. salt	for a 9″ double crust

Slip the skins from the grapes. Set the skins aside, but do not discard. Cook the grapes until soft, but do not boil. Put the grapes through a sieve or food mill, and discard the seeds.

In a mixing bowl, stir together the skins, juice, sugar, flour, salt, and lemon juice.

Roll out the bottom crust. Pour the grape filling into the shell.

Roll out the top crust. Cut into 1/2″ strips. Make a latticed top crust. Place 7-8 strips parallel to and about equidistant from each other on top of the filling, making certain that the ends of the strips lap over the rim of the pie pan. Weave the remaining 7-8 strips by criss-crossing across the original strips.

Bake at 350° F. for 50 minutes.

COCONUT CUSTARD CRUSTLESS PIE

3 eggs
1 c. raw sugar
1/3 c. whole wheat flour
1 1/2 c. milk
1 t. vanilla

3 T. butter, melted
1 t. baking powder
1 1/2 c. freshly grated
  coconut

Preheat the oven to 350° F. Butter a 9″ pie pan.

In a medium-sized bowl, beat the eggs until they are light. Stir in the remaining ingredients in the order in which they are listed. Pour into the buttered pie pan.

Bake for 40 minutes or until done. When a sharp knife inserted in the center of the pie comes out clean, the pie is done. Serve warm.

BROWN RICE PUDDING
(serves 3-4)

1 1/2 c. cooked
  brown rice
2 c. milk
1/4 t. salt

1/4 c. raw sugar
1/4 c. raisins
1/2 t. vanilla
1/4 t. nutmeg

Preheat the oven to 300° F.

Combine all ingredients in a 1 quart casserole and stir.

Bake for 45 minutes. Stir once, about 15 minutes after placing the casserole in the oven.

(*Note:* Uncooked brown rice should not be used for rice pudding because it takes too many hours to cook.)

PERSIMMON PUDDING

2 c. persimmon pulp
2 eggs
2/3 c. honey
1/2 t. salt
1/4 c. melted butter

2 t. baking powder
1 c. whole wheat flour
2 c. milk
1 t. cinnamon
1/4 t. nutmeg

Prepare the persimmon pulp by putting ripe persimmons through a sieve or colander.

Preheat the oven to 325° F. Butter a 9-inch square baking pan.

In a large mixing bowl, beat the eggs with the persimmon. Stir in the remaining ingredients.

Pour the pudding into the buttered pan. Bake for 1 hour or until a knife inserted in the center comes out clean. Serve warm or cold.

ORANGE CUSTARD

6 eggs
2/3 c. raw sugar
2 T. grated orange rind

1 1/2 c. fresh orange juice
1 c. heavy cream

Preheat the oven to 400° F.

Beat the eggs well. Add the sugar and stir until it is dissolved. Stir in the remaining ingredients.

Pour the mixture in an ungreased 2-quart casserole.

Place the casserole in a pan of water in the oven. Bake for about 1 hour or until a knife inserted in the center comes out clean.

DATE NUT PUDDING

1 c. dates, finely chopped
1 c. boiling water
1 c. raw sugar
1 egg
2 T. liquid oil

1 T. lemon juice
1/2 t. salt
1 1/2 t. baking powder
3/4 c. whole wheat flour
1 c. nuts, chopped

Preheat the oven to 350° F. Grease and flour a 9″ square pan.

Pour boiling water over the dates and set aside to cool.

In a medium-sized bowl, beat the sugar, egg, oil, and lemon juice. Add the cooled date mixture, and mix well. Stir in the salt, baking powder, flour, and nuts. Mix well.

Pour the batter into the greased pan. Bake for 25 minutes or until done.

BREAD PUDDING

4 c. warm milk
2 T. butter
2 c. stale bread or cake,
  cut into cubes
2/3 c. honey

3 eggs, beaten
1 c. seedless raisins
1/2 t. nutmeg
1 t. cinnamon
1 T. grated lemon rind

Butter a 9-inch square baking pan.

Add the milk and butter to a large bowl and allow the butter to dissolve. Add the bread cubes and let stand for 5-10 minutes to allow the bread to absorb the milk. Stir in the remaining ingredients.

Preheat the oven to 350° F.

Bake for 1 hour or until a knife inserted in the center comes out clean.

APPLE CRISP

4 c. apples,
    peeled and sliced
3 T. raw sugar
1/4 t. cinnamon
1 c. whole wheat flour
3/4 c. raw sugar
	1/4 t. salt
	1/4 t. cinnamon
	1 t. baking powder
	1 egg
	1/3 c. butter,
	    melted and cooled

Preheat the oven to 350° F.

Place the apples in an ungreased 9-inch baking dish. Sprinkle 3 tablespoons raw sugar and 1/4 teaspoon cinnamon over the apples.

In a mixing bowl, stir together the flour, 3/4 cup sugar, salt, 1/4 teaspoon cinnamon, and baking powder. Add the egg and stir with a fork until the mixture is crumbly. Sprinkle over the apples.

Pour the butter evenly over the top of the flour mixture.

Bake for 30 minutes.

FRUIT COBBLER

1/2 c. boiling water
3 c. sliced peaches
    or pitted cherries
3/4 c. raw sugar
1/2 t. nutmeg
1 c. whole wheat flour
2 T. raw sugar
	2 t. baking powder
	1/4 t. salt
	1 t. vanilla extract
	1/4 c. butter,
	    melted and cooled
	1/2 c. milk

Preheat the oven to 350° F.

Combine the boiling water, fruit, 3/4 cup sugar, and nutmeg in a bowl and let stand.

In a medium-sized mixing bowl, stir together the flour, 2 T. sugar, baking powder, and salt. Add the vanilla, butter, and milk and stir just to moisten the dry ingredients. Do not beat.

Pour the batter into an 8-inch square pan. Pour the fruit mixture gently and evenly over the batter.

Bake for 30 minutes or until done. Serve hot.

CHAPTER 10

WHEATLESS BAKING

THE IMPORTANCE OF gluten in bread baking, particularly the type of gluten found in wheat, has already been discussed. There are some people, however, who are allergic to wheat. More specifically, they are allergic to some of the substances which comprise the gluten in wheat. Consequently, it is necessary for them to avoid wheat products. This includes such obvious things as breads, cakes, pies, and rolls, and some less obvious products as spaghetti, wheat cereals, macaroni, crackers, etc.

It is important to realize that the adverse reaction to wheat products is really a reaction to the constituents of the gluten, namely gliadin. This fact has several implications. First, since gliadin is found only in the gluten of wheat flour (it is the substance which gives wheat flour its elastic properties), other gluten-containing flours, such as rye, can probably be used safely. Second, high protein bread products will cause the allergic individual more difficulty since their higher protein content is attributable to the fact that they contain more gluten (gluten is protein). Third, "wheatless" breads purchased in stores may cause allergic reactions since gluten may have been added to give the flour used the proper handling and rising qualities. Finally, since the allergic reaction is caused by the gluten, there is no need and no reason for avoiding wheat germ and bran. They are both healthful substances and should be included in the diet regardless of any allergy to gluten. Both the germ and the bran are gluten free.

This chapter provides a number of recipes for wheatless breads. The taste and texture of these breads will differ from that of wheat bread. On the one hand, they provide a substitute for wheat breads for those who must avoid wheat. On the other, they add variety and a new taste dimension in baking.

Scattered throughout the book are a number of wheatless recipes besides the ones in this chapter. Baked goods leavened with baking powder find greater success with non-wheat flours than do yeast-leavened products because non-yeast goods do not depend on a highly developed gluten for leavening. Rye flour is particularly good in quick breads, cakes, and cookies, and may be substituted for wheat flour in those sections.

100% WHOLE RYE BREAD
(one large loaf)

1 T. dry yeast
1 3/4 c. warm water
2 T. raw sugar
2 T. milk powder

1 t. salt
1 T. liquid oil
1 T. caraway seeds
4 1/2 - 5 c. whole rye flour

Grease one large loaf pan (9" x 5" x 2 3/4").

Sprinkle the yeast over warm water in a large mixing bowl. Allow the yeast to dissolve, about 5 minutes. Stir in the sugar, milk powder, salt, oil, and caraway seeds. Slowly add the flour until the dough stiffens and pulls away from the side of the bowl.

Turn the dough out on a floured board and knead until it feels elastic and springs back at the touch.

Shape the dough and place in the loaf pan. Brush the top with liquid oil, cover with a clean dish cloth and set in a warm place. Let the dough rise until it is about 3/4 inch above the rim of the pan.

Preheat the oven to 350° F.

Bake for 50 minutes or until done.

BARLEY-RYE BREAD
(one large loaf)

1 t. dry yeast
1/4 c. warm water
2 T. raw sugar
1/4 c. liquid oil
1/2 t. salt

1 T. baking powder
1 1/2 c. milk
2 c. barley flour
2 c. whole rye flour

Preheat the oven to 350° F. Grease one large loaf pan (9" x 5" x 2 3/4").

In a small bowl or cup, combine the yeast and warm water. Allow the yeast to dissolve, about 5 minutes.

In a large mixing bowl, stir the sugar and oil. Add the salt, baking powder, milk, and yeast. Stir in the barley and rye flours.

Pour the batter into the greased pan.

Bake for 1 hour or until done.

YANKEE CORN BREAD

2 1/2 c. cornmeal, plain
3 T. soy flour
2 1/2 T. raw sugar
1 t. salt
3 T. milk powder

2 t. baking powder
3 T. butter, melted
1 egg, beaten
1 1/4 c. water

Preheat the oven to 350° F. Grease a 9″ square baking dish.

In a large mixing bowl, combine the cornmeal, soy flour, sugar, salt, milk powder, and baking powder. Mix well. Stir in the remaining wet ingredients until well blended. Pour the batter into the greased baking dish.

Bake for 35-40 minutes or until done. When done, the crust will have a pale brown tinge.

(Note: This recipe will also make 12 muffins.)

SOUTHERN STYLE CORN BREAD

1 T. butter or lard
4 c. cornmeal, plain
1/2 t. salt

1 t. baking powder
2 eggs, lightly beaten
1 3/4 c. milk

Preheat the oven to 375° F.

Put the butter or lard in a 9″ square baking pan or a 10″ cast-iron skillet. Place the pan in the oven to melt the butter or lard, being careful that the butter does not brown.

In a large bowl, stir together the cornmeal, salt, and baking powder. Make a well in the center of the dry ingredients and add the eggs and milk. Stir until well blended.

Remove the baking pan from the oven. Gently tilt and shake the pan to coat the bottom and sides with the butter.

Pour the cornbread batter into the hot pan and place it in the oven. Bake for 30-35 minutes or until done.

FRESH CORN BREAD

1 1/2 c. cornmeal
1 t. salt
1 t. baking soda
1/4 t. freshly ground
   pepper
1/2 c. milk

1/4 c. butter, melted
2 eggs, beaten
1 c. fresh corn,
   scraped
1/4 c. onions,
   finely minced

Preheat the oven to 375° F. Butter an 8-inch square baking pan.

Stir together the dry ingredients. Stir in the remaining ingredients.

Pour the batter into the buttered baking pan.

Bake for 45 minutes or until done.

SOY MUFFINS
(one dozen muffins)

1 c. soy flour
1 c. whole rye flour
1 T. baking powder
1/2 t. salt
1/4 c. wheat germ

2 T. honey
1 egg, beaten
2 T. butter, melted
1 1/4 c. water

Preheat the oven to 350° F. Grease 12 muffin cups.

In a 1 1/2 quart mixing bowl, stir together the dry ingredients.

In a separate bowl, stir the liquid ingredients. Pour the liquid into the dry ingredients. Stir.

Pour the batter into the muffin tins, filling them about 3/4 full.

Bake for 20 minutes.

BANANA NUT BREAD
(one large loaf)

1/3 c. butter	1/2 t. salt
3 T. molasses	2 t. baking powder
1/4 c. honey	1/4 c. soy flour
2 eggs	1 3/4 c. whole rye flour
1 c. bananas, mashed	1/2 c. nuts, chopped
(about 2 medium bananas)	1 t. lemon rind, grated

Preheat the oven to 350° F. Grease a large loaf pan (9" x 5" x 2 3/4").

In a large mixing bowl, cream the butter, molasses, and honey. Beat in the eggs and bananas. Add the remaining ingredients and mix thoroughly.

Pour into the greased loaf pan and bake for 45-50 minutes or until done.

HONEY RYE LOAF
(one large loaf)

2 T. butter	1/2 t. salt
2 eggs	1 T. baking powder
1 c. honey	2 1/2 c. whole rye flour
1/3 c. milk	1/2 c. nuts, chopped
2 T. grated lemon rind	(optional)

Preheat the oven to 325° F. Butter a large loaf pan (9" x 5" x 2 3/4").

Beat the butter and the eggs. Stir in the honey and blend it in well. Add the remaining ingredients and mix well.

Pour the batter into the buttered loaf pan.

Bake for 50-60 minutes or until done.

SOY LOAF
(one medium loaf)

2/3 c. raw sugar
2 eggs
1/2 t. salt
1 T. baking powder

3/4 c. orange juice
1 c. soy flour
1 c. whole rye flour

Preheat the oven to 325° F. Grease a medium loaf pan (8″ x 4″ x 2 3/4″).

Beat the sugar and eggs until well blended. Stir in the remaining ingredients and mix well.

Pour the batter into the greased pan.

Bake for 50-60 minutes or until done.

ORANGE RYE POUND CAKE

1/2 lb. butter (1 cup)
1/2 lb. raw sugar (1 cup)
1/2 lb. eggs (4 large)
1 T. grated orange rind

1/2 t. salt
1 t. baking powder
1/2 lb. whole rye flour
    (2 cups)

Preheat the oven to 325° F. Butter a large loaf pan (9″ x 5″ x 2-3/4″).

Cream the butter, add the sugar, and beat well. Add the eggs, beating them in one at a time. Stir in the orange rind, salt, baking powder, and rye flour. Beat vigorously for about a minute.

Pour the batter into the buttered loaf pan. Bake for one hour or until done.

PINEAPPLE CAKE ROLL

2 c. crushed pineapple,
  cooked and unsweetened
1/3 c. raw sugar
3 eggs, separated
1/3 c. raw sugar

2 T. pineapple juice
1/2 t. salt
1 t. baking powder
1 c. whole rye flour

Preheat the oven to 375° F.

Drain the pineapple, then spread it on the bottom of a 9″ x 13″ baking pan. Sprinkle 1/3 cup raw sugar over the pineapple.

Beat together the egg yolks and 1/3 cup raw sugar. Stir in the remaining ingredients and mix well.

Beat the egg whites until stiff, but not dry. Fold the egg whites into the cake batter until it is well blended.

Spread the batter evenly over the pineapple.

Bake for 17-20 minutes or until done.

Loosen the cake from the sides of the pan with a spatula or knife. Turn the cake upside down on a clean dish cloth.

Gently roll the cake along the shorter side to make a cake roll 9 inches long.

Wrap in a clean dish cloth and allow to cool.

RICE COOKIES
(about 24 soft cookies)

1/3 c. liquid oil
1/3 c. raw sugar
1 egg
1/4 t. salt

1/2 t. almond
  or vanilla extract
1 t. baking powder
1 1/4 c. brown rice flour

Preheat the oven to 350° F. Grease a cookie sheet.

In a medium-sized bowl, stir the oil, sugar, and egg. Add the remaining ingredients and mix well.

Drop the dough by the heaping teaspoonful onto the cookie sheet.

Bake for 10-12 minutes or until lightly browned.

CORNMEAL COOKIES
(about 24 crisp cookies)

1/2 c. butter	1/4 t. salt
1/2 c. raw sugar	1 t. baking powder
1 egg	2 T. soy flour
1 t. grated orange rind	1 1/3 c. cornmeal

Preheat the oven to 350° F. Grease two cookie sheets.

In a medium-sized mixing bowl, cream the butter and sugar. Beat in the egg and orange rind. Stir in the remaining dry ingredients.

Form the cookie dough into balls about 3/4" in diameter. Place on cookie sheets about 3" apart. Flatten the balls of dough until about 1/4" thick.

Bake for 7-8 minutes or until lightly browned.

NO-WHEAT OATMEAL COOKIES
(about 30 crisp cookies)

2/3 c. liquid oil	1 t. baking powder
2/3 c. raw sugar	2/3 c. whole rye flour
1 egg	1/3 c. barley flour
1/2 t. salt	1 1/2 c. rolled oats, uncooked

Preheat the oven to 350° F. Lightly grease two cookie sheets.

Stir together the oil, sugar, and egg. Add the salt, baking powder, and flours. Mix in the oats and blend well.

Drop by the heaping teaspoonful onto the cookie sheets.

Bake for 10-12 minutes or until lightly browned.

COCO-CORN PIE

1/4 c. cornmeal
1 1/2 c. milk
3 eggs
1/2 c. honey

1 t. vanilla
3 T. butter, melted
1 1/2 c. freshly grated
   coconut

Stir the cornmeal and milk in a saucepan. Stirring constantly, cook over a medium low flame until thick. Allow to cool.

Preheat the oven to 325° F. Generously butter a 9″ pie pan.

Beat the cornmeal and eggs. Add the remaining ingredients and stir well.

Pour the mixture into the buttered pan.

Bake for 45-50 minutes.

APPLE CRUNCH

3 c. apples,
   peeled and sliced
1 T. lemon juice
3 T. raw sugar
1/4 t. cinnamon
1/2 c. brown rice flour

3/4 c. rolled oats,
   uncooked
2/3 c. raw sugar
1/2 t. salt
1 t. baking powder
1/3 c. butter, melted

Preheat the oven to 350° F.

Place the apples in an ungreased 1-quart casserole. Sprinkle the lemon juice, 3 tablespoons raw sugar, and cinnamon over the apples.

In a mixing bowl, stir together the remaining ingredients. Sprinkle the mixture over the apples.

Bake for 30-35 minutes.

HONEY RICE PUDDING
(serves 3-4)

1 1/2 c. brown rice, cooked
1/4 c. brown rice flour
1/2 c. honey
2 c. milk, warm

1/4 t. salt
2 T. grated orange rind
1/4 t. cinnamon
1/4 c. raisins (optional)

Preheat the oven to 325° F.

Stir together all of the ingredients in a 1-quart casserole.

Place the casserole in the oven and bake for about 45 minutes.

APPLE PUDDING

3/4 c. raw sugar
1/4 c. butter, melted
1 egg
1/2 t. cinnamon
1/4 t. nutmeg

1/4 t. salt
1 t. baking soda
1 c. whole rye flour
1/2 c. nuts or raisins
2 1/2 - 3 c. apples, chopped

Preheat the oven to 375° F. Butter an 8-inch square pan.

Stir together the sugar, butter, and egg. Add the dry ingredients and stir in. Add the nuts or raisins and chopped apples.

Pour the mixture into the buttered pan.

Bake for 30 minutes or until apples are soft.

INDIAN PUDDING
(serves 4-6)

1 qt. skim or whole milk	1/2 t. salt
1/2 c. cornmeal, plain	1 t. cinnamon
2 T. butter, melted	1/4 t. ginger, powdered
1/2 c. honey	2 eggs

Combine the milk and cornmeal in a 3-quart saucepan. Stirring constantly, heat over a low flame or over hot water in a double boiler until the mixture thickens, about 20 minutes. Remove from the heat and allow to cool slightly.

Preheat the oven to 325° F. Butter a 1 1/2 quart casserole or baking dish.

In a medium-sized bowl, add the butter, honey, salt, cinnamon, ginger, and eggs. Beat well. Pour the egg mixture into the cornmeal, and stir until well blended.

Pour the pudding into the buttered dish, and place in a pan of hot water in the oven. Bake for about 1 hour or until a toothpick inserted in the center comes out clean. Serve warm.

BUCKWHEAT CAKES
(serves 4)

2 1/2 c. buckwheat flour	2 T. molasses
2 1/2 c. milk	1 1/2 T. baking powder
1 T. liquid oil	1/2 t. salt
2 T. raw sugar	1 egg, beaten

Heat a lightly greased griddle.

Combine all of the ingredients in a large mixing bowl. Beat until well blended.

Pour or spoon the batter into cakes of desired size on the hot griddle. Turn the cakes when the bubbles begin to retain their holes.

APPENDIX

SOURCES
OF NATURAL FOODS

MAIL ORDER SUPPLIERS

Arrowhead Mills, Inc.; P.O. Box 866, Hereford, Texas 79045

Barth's of Long Island; 270 West Merrick Rd., Valley Stream, L.I., New York 11582

Better Foods Foundation, Inc.; 200 N. Washington St., Greencastle, Pennsylvania 17225

Brownville Mills; Brownville, Nebraska 68321

Chico-San; 1262 Humboldt, Chico, California 95926

Dietrich's Organic Farm; R.R. #1, Genoa, Ohio 43430

El Molino Mills; 3060 W. Valley Blvd., Alhambra, California 91803

The Great Valley Mills; Quakertown, Bucks County, Pennsylvania 18951

Jaffe Brothers; 28560 Lilac Rd., Valley Center, California 92082

The Natural Development Co.; Box 215, Bainbridge, Pennsylvania 17502

Mel Cordes; Henning, Minnesota 56551

Nature Food Centres; 292 Main St., Cambridge, Mass. 02139

Natural Sales Co.; Box 25, Pittsburgh, Pa. 15230

Northern Health Foods; Box 66, 13 S. 4th St., Moorhead, Minnesota 56560

Organic Foods and Gardens; 1384 S. Rice Rd., Ojai, California 93023

Sierra Natural Foods; 2408 26th St., Sacramento, California 95818

Sioux Millers; R.R. 1, Whiting, Iowa 51063

Stur-Dee Health Products; Island Park, New York 11558

Walnut Acres; Penns Creek, Pennsylvania 17862

Wesley K. Wilson; Box 481, LaCrosse, Kansas 67548

LOCAL SOURCES

General Nutrition Center Stores, 164 stores in 32 States

Health Food Stores

Natural Foods Co-Ops

Local Organic Farmers

_____

The Organic Directory (Rodale Press, Inc., 33 E. Minor St., Emmaus, Pennsylvania 18049) may be very helpful in locating nearby sources of natural foods.

INDEX

FAVORITE BREAD RECIPES

FAVORITE ROLL RECIPES

FAVORITE CAKE RECIPES

FAVORITE COOKIE RECIPES

FAVORITE PIE AND PUDDINGS RECIPES

FAVORITE SUPPLIERS